STOP Dating Jerks!

The Smart Woman's Guide to Breaking the Pattern & FINDING THE LOVE OF YOUR LIFE

Dr. Joseph Nowinski

Associate Adjunct Professor of Psychology at the University of Connecticut

SUNRISE
River Press

Sunrise River Press
39966 Grand Avenue
North Branch, MN 55056
Phone: 651-277-1400 or 800-895-4585
Fax: 651-277-1203
www.sunriseriverpress.com

Dedication

For Terri, with love

Edit by Karin Craig
Layout by Monica Bahr

ISBN 978-1-934716-04-5
Item No. SRP604

Library of Congress Cataloging-in-Publication Data

Nowinski, Joseph.
  Stop dating jerks! : the smart woman's guide to breaking the pattern and finding the love of your life / by Joseph Nowinski.
     p. cm.
  Includes index.
  ISBN 978-1-934716-04-5
  1. Dating (Social customs) 2. Men—Psychology. 3. Man-woman relationships. I. Title.
  HQ801.N65 2010
  646.7'7082—dc22
                                        2009024342

Printed in USA
10 9 8 7 6 5 4 3 2 1

TABLE OF CONTENTS

A Book That Doesn't Sell You Short

(Or Sell You at All!)

Is he eligible, and is he worth pursuing?

If you are ready to ask yourself the above question—not just the first half, but the second half as well—then this book will be helpful to you.

This is a book for single women who are looking for a long-term relationship. If you are such a woman, there is a good chance you've already done some reading and found that some of the most common advice for achieving your goal is disappointing—perhaps even depressing. You may have tried following such typical advice as, "Look good, be perky, and be where the men are."

Or, as one book urges, you may have come up with a list of your best qualities, and then tried presenting yourself as "an attractive package," as if you were a car or a flat-screen television—and as though you were trying to inspire a man to acquire you! Many books on dating repeat this same basic advice in slightly different ways. I call this the *marketing approach* to finding a man.

Avoiding the Marketing Approach

There's a problem with the marketing approach. It doesn't help a woman decide whether a man who seems interested in her (and vice versa) is actually worth pursuing. In other words, the goal of marketing yourself is to make you an attractive package, period.

If that's your sole objective, fine. But what most women want is not just to attract men, but to be able to identify one who may be a potential partner. The marketing approach reduces you to a commodity and allows men to more or less sit back and be choosy, when it's just as important for you to be choosy. The marketing approach can easily lead you to feel that you are somehow defective or inferior if your "marketing plan" is not successful. Jackie Lee Thomas, writing about her venture into the Internet dating scene in the December 3, 2007, issue of *Newsweek*, described her experience with the marketing approach:

As quickly as the attractive snapshot faces had appeared, they likewise vanished into the silent cosmos of the Internet. I was left with pensive hands on the keyboard wondering what had happened. Had I seemed desperate or, worse, pathetic at 48? Maybe my teeth weren't straight enough. Maybe I couldn't pass off those wrinkles as smile lines after all. The doubts came flooding in like a summer downpour.

What women don't need is another book that repeats the obvious: It's important for a woman (as well as for a man) who is interested in dating to put some effort into looking her best and putting her best foot forward. In other words, what you don't need is another book about how to market yourself. You most likely already know plenty about that.

A Better Way: Using the Selective Approach

Fortunately, there is an alternative to the marketing approach. I call it the *selective approach*. It's based on the simple idea that what single women can use is a book that offers the following:

- It is grounded in solid information about male psychology and personality development.
- It helps them size up men and identify the ones to avoid.
- It includes critical tests they can use to help separate potential partners from likely heartaches.
- It gives advice on how to develop a relationship with a man who may be imperfect but nevertheless has potential.

This book offers you all these things. It is for women who, despite their best intentions, have wasted time, money, and emotional energy trying to find their match using the marketing approach. They may have spent money on a dating service or wasted precious time responding to Internet singles listings, only to find that the men they ended up dating turned out not to be "as advertised."

It's not for lack of intelligence that women pursue what amounts to dead ends, so much as the fact that you simply can't judge a book by its cover. And that's exactly what the marketing approach, dating services, and Internet dating sites focus on—attractive "covers" that aim to catch your interest.

The women who will find this book most helpful—as well as those who are likely to succeed in finding and keeping a good man—are women who have come to the conclusion that it is important to take time to get to know a man before getting too serious. That is, to look inside the cover.

It is important to decide if there is enough potential in a man to make it worth putting in the effort needed to build a relationship—as opposed to trying to transform every man who shows an interest into Mr. Right.

If you can identify with either or both of these two frequent mistakes—either rushing in or trying too hard to make a lemon into lemonade—then you will find this book illuminating. Congratulate yourself on being mature and thoughtful enough to take responsibility for your choices in men, as well as acknowledging any mistakes you've made in the past. Now it's time to be more educated and thoughtful as you move forward.

This is not a book about how to attract a man (*any* man), what to do if and when you realize that your relationship is in deep trouble, or how to get rid of (or get over) a bad relationship. Instead, this book gives you the tools you need to identify different types of personality problems in men and to assess how severe a man's problem may be. Once you have this knowledge, you can decide for yourself whether a man's issues are so severe that it would be pointless to go further, or whether his flaws are within an allowable range. If the latter seems to be the case, this book gives you advice on how not to contribute to a man's limitations—and how to help him get over them.

Many books on dating, intentionally or not, sell readers short when they take the marketing approach. This book doesn't sell you short. In fact, it doesn't ask you to sell yourself at all. On the contrary, it offers a totally different perspective on dating.

Rather than encouraging you to market yourself, this book guides you toward being more discriminating in deciding which of the men you meet are worth putting some effort into, versus knowing when to move on. It is based on stories that many single women have told me, most of which have a common bottom line: These women's greatest regrets were not that they could not *find* a man, but that they had wasted so much time and energy trying to make a basically bad (or mediocre) relationship work. If this describes your experience, then this is the book for you.

Finding Mr. Wrong: The Marketing Approach

Stop Dating Jerks! is organized in four parts. This first part takes a critical look at the advice that is most commonly offered to women about how to attract men and make one fall in love with you. This advice—which millions of women, unfortunately, take to heart—is mostly based on stereotypes of men that turn out to be myths.

One such stereotype is that men pursue and commit themselves only to a woman who is mysterious, exotic, or hard to get. If she were to accept this stereotype as fact and try to follow this advice, a woman would have to become a modern-day Scheherazade, keeping her man interested by spinning a different yarn each night. Some women pursue a variation on this approach by changing their look on a regular basis. It's one thing to change your look to please yourself. But what sane woman would want to take on the burden of constantly looking different just to keep a man from turning to someone else?

Before I get to the issues of how to identify a good man and then how to keep him, let's take a look at how many women end up wasting lots of time pursuing several Mr. Wrongs, usually because they chose to take the marketing approach described in the Introduction. The advantage to looking at the mistakes described in Part One is simple: If you can identify with one or more of the common mistakes that women make when looking for a relationship, then that insight alone can help you avoid wasting valuable time and energy in the future—and very possibly, spare you considerable heartache.

Chapter One

Chemistry Lessons

Let's take a closer look at the idea that women seeking a relationship have a minute (or less) to catch a man's interest. If he passes you up after a mere sixty seconds, your potential relationship of a lifetime is over before it starts. This idea has been put forth strongly in at least one book about dating. But is it true? And if it were true, what are the implications for single women?

The Truth About Chemistry

People who embrace this belief often also say that they believe in the power of that age-old force called *chemistry*. Some go so far as to argue that when you and Mr. Right meet, you'll both know that you were meant for each another virtually instantaneously. Some people refer to this as *synchronicity*.

As romantically appealing as this notion may be, on a practical level it places a heavy burden on single women to arouse a man's interest as quickly as possible—in other words, to market themselves very effectively. It drives them to spend a fortune on clothing and makeup, to refine their ability to engage men in conversation, and to create Internet descriptions that make them sound as attractive and interesting as possible, while at the same time being careful not to violate the "one minute or less" rule. No wonder most people quickly become cynical about trying to meet people over the Internet, through dating services, or through the singles scene.

What does all this effort to make a good (and fast) first impression boil down to? Is it really a matter of finding your perfect match—your soul mate—in a minute or less? Or is it a matter of finding someone *attractive* in sixty seconds or less? I think it's the latter. To be even more specific, in most cases, I believe that chemistry boils down to what I would call "sexual/personality attraction."

A man who meets a woman and immediately begins to pursue her is most likely *not* doing so because he believes he's just found his lifelong soul mate. Rather, the chances are that he thinks this is a woman who is attractive and whose outward personality appeals to him. For instance, she may have a good sense of humor or be flirtatious or even sarcastic. For an example of the latter, see the movie *The Big Sleep,* starring Humphrey Bogart and Lauren Bacall. Bogart is clearly attracted to Bacall, not only because of her good looks, but also because she has a charming, sarcastic side. Based on these two qualities—good looks and intriguing outward personality—a man decides he might be interested in a woman he's just met. Period. No lifelong soul mating implied!

Chemistry as defined here is real, and it may be important. Many people believe that it is an essential first ingredient for a lasting relationship. That said, there is no way to know whether chemistry will lead to a one-night stand or to marriage. In fact, sexual desire being the potent instinctual force that it is, a woman is much better off assuming that the man would probably just like to have sex with her.

Case Study

Maria and Mitchell: The Perils of Speed-Dating

Here is what happened to one woman who allowed herself to believe too naively and completely in the power of chemistry and acted impulsively on that belief. Maria, age 32, was born and raised in a foreign country. After graduating from college with honors, she came to the United States to pursue graduate studies in the medical sciences. The daughter of two successful professionals, she had always been bright and successful academically, though she tended to be modest and downplayed her talents and accomplishments.

The Background: Maria and John

Shortly after she completed her doctorate, Maria broke off a three-year relationship with John, a man she described as intelligent, pleasant, and easy to be with, but notably lacking in passion and motivation. He had basically lived off of Maria for most of their time together, making several false starts to pursue some sort of career, but never staying with any one of them for longer than a few months. Occasionally, he would clean the apartment or make a meal, but in general, Maria had no idea how John spent his time. Meanwhile, she worked pretty much seven days a week, as do most doctoral students.

The breakup was easier than Maria expected. She anticipated a good deal of resistance, particularly since John had no visible means of support and, as far as she knew, had nowhere to go. But when she sat down with him and had the heart-to-heart talk she'd rehearsed in her mind a hundred times, he essentially said, "Okay," went into the bedroom to fill a duffel bag with clothes, and left.

Two days later, John called to say he would be back over the weekend to pick up the remainder of his things. When he showed up, he acted as if everything was just fine. He smiled and even gave Maria a little hug. Baffled and curious about where John had gone when he left, she asked him. She was stunned to learn that he was "crashing" in the apartment of his former girlfriend.

John's cavalier attitude knocked the wind out of Maria's sails. She had put a great deal of effort into the relationship, and expected him to value it as well—even be devastated at the loss of her companionship. His reaction, instead, led her to conclude that she meant very little to him. She distracted herself by finishing her dissertation and then applied for and won a postdoctoral research fellowship. She redecorated her apartment, spent some time reconnecting with female friends, and planned an extended trip abroad to visit her family.

A New Dating Technique

When she returned from her trip, Maria came to terms with the breakup and decided it was time to begin dating again. A friend told her about a new dating technique that she'd tried several times. *Speed-dating* involved about a dozen single men and women pairing off sequentially for five minutes, after which a buzzer would go off and it was time to meet a new partner. At the end of an hour, participants would indicate which (if any) of the twelve singles they'd be interested in dating. They were then free to pursue or not pursue any "chemistry" they'd discovered through the speed-dating.

Despite the fact that Maria was skeptical of speed-dating, she decided to keep an open mind. She was intrigued when her friend explained that research showed people could tell if they were truly meant for one another within a few minutes of meeting. Maria's friend insisted that she could always tell if she was interested in a man (and vice versa) pretty quickly. In part, she saw speed-dating as a way for her and the men she met to decide quickly if they wanted to date. On another level, she confessed that she believed she could meet her soul mate this way. Deep down, she held on to the romantic notion that she and her soul mate would recognize each other instantaneously when they met.

Looking back on the three years she felt she'd wasted with John, Maria concluded that she had nothing to lose by going along with her friend. She told herself it might even be fun.

When the fateful evening arrived, Maria's friend helped her pick out what clothes to wear. She also advised Maria to put on just a little extra makeup. Then she shared some of the strategies she developed in the course of speed-dating several times before. She explained that it was important to ask open-ended questions and to express interest in each man she met: "This book I read said that all men basically want to talk about themselves. So if you want to attract a man, act like you're really interested in everything he has to say."

Maria and Mitchell

A dark, handsome man of Mediterranean descent, Mitchell was the fifth man that Maria met during her one and only speed-dating experience.

She felt instantly attracted to Mitchell, much more so than to the other men she'd met, and the attraction seemed to be mutual. Another reason she liked Mitchell was that they seemed to get comfortable talking to each other about themselves almost instantly and without effort. She had followed her friend's advice and expressed interest in what the men she met had to say, but she felt that Mitchell was equally interested in what she had to say. Maria was highly educated, and she felt that men were sometimes intimidated by her. But not Mitchell.

After the speed-dating event, Maria and Mitchell both indicated that they wanted to see each other again. They went out for coffee the next night and ended up talking into the wee hours. Maria learned that Mitchell had dropped out of college, worked for a real-estate firm selling commercial leases, and was taking college courses at night. His long-term goal was to get a degree in accounting and become a certified public accountant. In comparison to John, Maria found Mitchell's ambition refreshing and attractive.

"We became an item very quickly," said Maria. "On our second date he told me that he loved me, and that we were meant to be together. And then he said he wanted me to be the mother of his children! He was very passionate." Maria naturally felt flattered by the intensity of Mitchell's feelings; she was definitely attracted to him. However, when he started talking about having children on their second date, her initial reaction was to put on the brakes. After all, she reasoned, they hardly knew each other. Her friend, however, was very excited for her. She told Maria that this was what falling in love was all about, and that it could be that she and Mitchell found their respective soul mates.

Barely three months after meeting Mitchell, Maria was pregnant. To her surprise and chagrin, the initial reaction from Mitchell—the man who'd said on their second date that he wanted Maria to be the mother of his children—was not what she expected. Though he didn't say it directly, she felt that his body language revealed some ambivalence. The pregnancy moved ahead without incident, and Maria gave birth to a healthy, beautiful girl they named Isabel. Maria and Mitchell were married a month after Isabel's birth.

Was It All Too Fast?

A year later, Maria was in therapy, feeling depressed and complaining of anxiety attacks. Professionally, she was as successful as ever. She had been the one of fifty applicants accepted for a position in the medical research division of a major corporation. On the one hand, her work, which she found both challenging and rewarding, made Maria feel that she was helping to make the world a better place for her daughter. On the other hand, the pressures on a new researcher in the competitive health-care industry were significant. Maria was expected not only to pursue original research, but also, much like an academic researcher, to publish and present papers at professional conferences.

Maria's depression and bouts with anxiety began soon after she, Mitchell, and Isabel moved and she began her new job. She felt ambivalent about leaving Isabel every day for fairly long hours at the lab. Mitchell, meanwhile, decided he didn't want to pursue either real-estate or public accounting after all, and that in any case finishing college would take too long. Instead, he said he wanted to build a business of his own, selling items over the Internet. He wasn't yet sure what he wanted to sell, but he had busied himself reading books about how to start an online business and how to create and maintain a Website.

Maria initially took comfort in the idea that Mitchell would be at home with Isabel, but then one day he told her that he wanted to be able to focus on his business more instead of being tied down by a one-year-old-child's constant needs and demands. So they hired a part-time nanny, who came to the house every morning for five hours after Maria left for work, allowing Mitchell to close the door to his home office and pursue his business. This added expense made money tight, increasing the level of tension between Maria and Mitchell. They had rarely argued before, but since the nanny arrived, the frequency of little spats between them picked up noticeably.

The stress that finally sent Maria over the edge—and that triggered her first anxiety attack—was a two-week visit from her mother, which ended in open conflict between her mother and Mitchell. Maria's mother let it be known that as far as she was concerned, Mitchell was little more than a lazy dreamer, content to be supported by his wife. Maria explained that she didn't think that was true of Mitchell, but as an outside observer, her therapist was not convinced that her mother was entirely wrong. It seemed to the therapist that Maria might be one of those women who end up getting into relationships with what I call "beach boys," a type of man I'll describe later.

What ended up happening to Maria's marriage (they divorced) is less important right now than the fact that a key factor that contributed to her unhappy situation was her decision to place all her chips on a five-minute encounter. True enough, there was some chemistry between Maria and Mitchell. But did this chemistry mean that they had instantaneously discovered their soul mates?

Is it Synchronicity or Just Impulsiveness?

The truth about men—as opposed to the stereotype that they all make snap decisions about women—is that many will labor for days, weeks, or even months trying to decide whether to pursue a woman they're attracted to. These same men are also likely to labor over many other decisions: whether to buy a new car or high-definition television, where to go on vacation, and so on. Many of these men would make perfectly fine partners. They're just naturally cautious.

In contrast, the man who makes the snap decision that a woman he's just met is his long-sought soul mate is apt to be someone who generally tends to be impulsive in how he approaches life and makes important decisions. Such men are likely to fall out of love as quickly as they fall into it. Typically, they are impulsive purchasers and poor savers. Like John and Mitchell, their lives often don't follow one path for very long. In a relationship with this kind of man, a woman is apt to find herself forced to take on the role of responsible adult, which puts her in a no-win "parental" position—hardly a good omen if you're looking for a long-term relationship.

A man may well know whether he is *attracted* to a woman within sixty seconds, but assuming that this attraction is a sign of lasting love or soul mating is usually a big mistake.

We've all heard stories of couples who say they knew they were meant for each other the first time they met. Perhaps such synchronicity does sometimes occur. My advice to single women is to avoid making commitments impulsively. I also advise against indulging in wishful thinking about a synchronicity scenario or believing that singles services are able to find your perfect match.

Don't Mistake Chemistry for Love

It's fine to feel intensely attracted to a man or to sense that he is equally attracted to you, even the very first time you meet. Take his signals as flattering. You're an adult, and you can decide for yourself if you want to act quickly on such chemistry, knowing that the relationship may very well be over soon after it begins. It's called a fling. Though some counselors seem clearly opposed to such behavior, I'd prefer to leave it up to an intelligent woman to make her own decision. But whatever you do, don't try to convince yourself that such attraction is a sign from above that you and Mr. Right have just found one another. As flattering as a quick pursuit might be, keep an open mind about men who may be more shy and deliberate about when and how they make a move. There are many men who may make a much better match in the long run.

Chapter Two

Choosy or Burned Out?

It has become commonplace to characterize single men as afraid of commitment, as though this were some new disease afflicting unmarried men. Indeed, men have sought counseling for this supposed illness. "Do you think I'm afraid of commitment?" they ask with a puzzled look on their faces. Or, "I've been told I'm afraid of commitment," they say with conviction, and then look at me as if they just told me that they were afraid of spiders and expected me to cure them.

As a rule, men are not innately afraid of commitment any more than women are. However, some men may become cautious or shy as a consequence of feeling burned.

Case Study

Joshua's Story: Caution on the Road to Lasting Happiness

Joshua was beginning to worry about his future. As he put it, "My biological clock is ticking." That phrase is more often associated with women, but it's a concept that applies to men as well. Joshua was referring to the fact that, at age 44, he still had not realized the dream of adult life that he had when he was a teenager. Back then, he envisioned himself being married with children and living a comfortable middle-class life. He could even picture it: a white wood-frame house on a couple of acres, a fireplace, maybe even a fenced-in yard for the kids and dog.

But that was not how things worked out. Joshua had at least four serious, long-term relationships, none of which led to his vision. In two cases the woman ended the relationship, and twice he called it quits himself. The last one, however, was by far the most painful breakup, because, unlike the other times, Joshua had gotten married, despite having reservations about the relationship from the beginning.

Life with Karen: Nice Guy Finishes Last

Karen, twice divorced and the single mother of a young son, told Joshua that one of her goals was to have a second child. Joshua signed on for this, as it fit in nicely with his own vision of a happy and fulfilling adulthood. The reservations he had about Karen revolved around his perception that she was someone who liked to run the show. She had strong opinions about almost everything and she asserted them, sometimes so forcefully that she came across as someone who believed hers were the only opinions that mattered.

Inwardly, Joshua chafed at this, but he did not like confrontation, so he tended to keep his disagreements to himself. Also, having dated so many women and feeling as frustrated as he did, he took to heart the advice of a good woman friend who suggested that maybe he was too fussy, and that what he needed to do was to realize that everyone had their flaws. So he decided to cut Karen a lot of slack when it came to being opinionated and tried to focus instead on her qualities that he liked.

Not long after they were married, Karen retracted earlier statements she'd made about buying a house together. Instead, she insisted that Joshua move into her house and that they split the expenses. The reason she gave was that this would be less disruptive to her son. Joshua gave in, though in his heart he would have liked the three of them to start family life together on a new footing.

Things went along reasonably well for the first year or so. During this time, Joshua continued to avoid arguing or disagreeing with Karen. This approach was reinforced on those few occasions when he did venture to disagree with her. Each time, he found that she was relentless in her efforts to convince him that she was right and he was wrong. By the time they celebrated their first anniversary, Joshua was aware that the price he paid for avoiding conflict was less and less communication with Karen. She commented on this on occasion—that Joshua talked to her less than he had in the past. Whenever she brought it up, he would just shrug his shoulders and say something to the effect that he was a person who just didn't have much to say. That, of course, was a lie, but Joshua much preferred being quiet over speaking up and risking an argument that he was sure to lose in the long run.

As unsatisfying as the lack of open communication in his marriage was to Joshua, he believed he could live with it. Unfortunately, that was not the only issue he had to deal with. Things between him and Karen took a distinct downhill turn as they struggled to get pregnant. Karen believed it was Joshua's fault, although medical tests were inconclusive and suggested only that his sperm count was toward the lower end of the normal range. Karen, meanwhile, was 37, and her doctor advised her that, although she was healthy, the chances of getting pregnant were slimmer after age 35.

When Karen brought up the idea of adoption, Joshua was ambivalent about it. "It wasn't that I felt I had to have my own kid," he explained, "so much as I was beginning to have reservations about the relationship. In particular, I was starting to get angry over how Karen had to have her own way when it came to even the smallest decisions about her son. I was pretty much on the outside looking in. I began to wonder what my role would be as a father. I could bite my lip when it came to her son, but I was sure I wouldn't be able to do that with a child I considered my own."

As time passed, the marriage showed more and more signs of strain as a result of Karen not getting pregnant and Joshua's hesitancy to pursue adoption. Spats became more frequent, as the two found themselves at a stalemate. "To me, it felt like Karen just had to have things her way," Joshua explained. "If I wanted something different, or even had a different opinion about something, I was wrong."

As unhappy as he was, when the divorce papers were handed to him, Joshua was pretty much devastated. Karen had initiated the divorce following a single session of marriage counseling, after which she told Joshua that she would not go back because the therapist "wasn't listening" to her.

A Slower Start with Brigitte

It was nearly two years before Joshua finally gave in to the coaxing of friends and began dating again, and soon he met Brigitte. As Joshua described it, meeting and getting to know Brigitte was not a matter of "chemistry" or impulsiveness on either of their parts. On the contrary, they dated for more than six months and had not yet been intimate other than for an occasional hug or kiss on the cheek.

On their first date, Brigitte told Joshua that she was dating another man and that she was not sure how that relationship would turn out. She enjoyed Joshua's company, she explained, but she did not feel comfortable being intimate with two men. However, she liked Joshua, and if he was up for seeing one another occasionally, she would like that.

This arrangement was okay with Joshua, at least at first. He felt that he'd been burned enough times that the idea of just being friends and having some fun with a woman might be the safer course for him. When he described the experiences he and Brigitte shared, though, it was apparent that they not only had a really good time together, but that they shared many common interests, had a similar sense of humor, and could talk about just about anything.

Joshua described Brigitte as very different from Karen in that she seemed quite tolerant of differences in people's opinions and tastes. At the same time, he recognized that their values and priorities were similar.

He readily admitted that he felt attracted to Brigitte, and that his feelings for her were growing. But he was not sure how she felt about him and was reluctant to ask. "If I tell her I'm attracted to her," he explained, "she could tell me that she doesn't feel the same. Where would that leave me?"

Joshua struggled for months with the idea of letting Brigitte know he was attracted to her. He wanted to tell her that he found her sexy, that he thought about being in a relationship with her, and even about having a child with her. He wanted to know if she felt anything more than friend-ship for him.

The reason for Joshua's hesitancy was obvious, yet he agreed with me that he had nothing to lose at this point by sharing his feelings since it was becoming increasingly apparent that the relationship could not go on much longer as it was. It would have to go in one direction or another, and sooner rather than later. It was now beginning to be uncomfortable for Joshua to spend a weekend with Brigitte and have a great time, but not be intimate and not know what was going on in the rest of her life. The issue of her other relationship had not come up between them for some time. He had no idea whether that relationship was still on, whether he might get an e-mail one day from Brigitte: "Just to let you know, I'm get-ting married next weekend. It's been fun. Have a great life!"

Joshua decided to write Brigitte a letter and share his feelings. "I don't want to do it in an e-mail," he said. "And somehow telling her over the phone or even in person feels like I'd be putting her on the spot." He felt that get-ting a letter would give her some time to reflect before responding. "Also," he said with a grin, "it's novel. Nobody actually writes letters anymore!"

Joshua sent me an e-mail to let me know that he'd mailed the letter. Five days passed, with no further word. I could only imagine what Joshua must be thinking and feeling. Then I got a message on my voice mail. It was from Joshua, and he sounded excited. "Brigitte left a message on my cell phone last night," he said. "I'd left my phone in the car and didn't get it until this morning. She said that it was the nicest letter she had ever gotten, and that she wanted to talk. She also said that she had ended that other rela-tionship a couple of months ago and was trying to decide when to tell me."

Joshua could be described as a man who became cautious as a result of his prior experiences. However, he was not a man who wanted women to market themselves to him. It was caution—not pickiness—that made him move slowly. In contrast to Joshua are men who could more accurately be described as relationship burnouts. Getting involved with a man who has suffered burnout, as opposed to a cautious man, is generally a mistake, but a situation that a surprising number of women fall into.

Sara and Tom: How Relationship Burnout Happens

Tom was also 44 years old. Like Joshua, he had also married and been divorced by a woman who was the single mother of a young son. Tom's marriage to Sara could best be described as an emotional roller coaster. Based on the way he described their day-to-day relationship, it was obvious that Tom lived his life walking on eggshells. Sara was extremely thin-skinned and sensitive. Her feelings were forever getting hurt by things that, from her point of view, were major acts of disrespect, insensitivity, or lack of love. From Tom's perspective, Sara tended to blow things out of proportion. She would also share with him her perceptions of how her family, friends, and co-workers treated her badly. Often, it was difficult for Tom to see the alleged offenses Sara was referring to, and he thought she was overreacting to normal human foibles or, at worst, innocent teasing. But he quickly learned that in Sara's view there were no unintentional acts—only insensitive, uncaring people.

Another issue for Tom was that if he did not get Sara's prior approval for even relatively minor decisions, he could be in for a confrontation that could last for days. He once came home with two bags of grass seed and a small shrub, thinking he would re-seed some bare patches in the back yard and replace a shrub that had died. Sara immediately confronted him, asking why he hadn't talked with her first about what kind of seed and shrub to buy. She then refused to talk to him until he returned the seeds and the shrub.

Although it's possible that Sara had some interest in gardening, you can imagine how reactions like hers to even such relatively minor issues could lead to a strained marriage. A good marriage is the epitome of the art of compromise, just as much as it is the epitome of a shared vision. On the one hand, if you want to plant a shrub that you like, is it really that important that I like it too? On the other hand, if you want to completely re-landscape our property, I would like to be included in the decision, as well as the subsequent planning.

Over their five years of marriage, Sara must have threatened Tom with divorce a hundred times. The trigger for these reactions was always her perception that he did not love or respect her. Sometimes he could see what he'd done to offend her but didn't believe his actions or words meant what she thought they meant. At other times, he frankly could not see what had offended her.

Sara asked Tom to leave on several occasions. Each time, he would pack a bag, move in with family or friends, and tell himself that it was over. His friends and family would agree and encourage him to move on with his life. Each time, however, Sara would initiate contact and they would reconcile. She'd explain that as frustrating as their marriage was for her, she truly loved Tom and felt committed to him. And so she would welcome him back with open arms, and all would be well for a while.

For his part, Tom tended to remember the good times that followed these separations more than the bad times that inevitably returned. Ironically, the more often he was threatened with divorce or asked to leave, the more committed Tom seemed to become to Sara. He was convinced that they loved each other, that every separation would be the last, and that each invitation to return would prove to be the doorway to everlasting happiness.

Naturally, when the final breakup came, it threw Tom for a loop. He couldn't believe it was really happening. Sara, who so often criticized others for being unfaithful, told him she had fallen in love with another man.

Again, when Tom left, his family and friends consoled him, telling him that he'd tried his best, but that the marriage just wasn't meant to be. He resigned himself to the divorce, but for a long time he felt as if he was in a life raft that had been cast adrift. He went through the motions of life, but without gusto. He kept his job as a teacher, but his colleagues and department head could not help remarking on his lack of enthusiasm.

The saying, "Once burned, twice shy," sums up Joshua's situation. It's easy to understand how men who have done a lot of unsuccessful dating or who have made commitments and then been rejected might become cautious or shy. But *relationship burnout* is a more apt term for what Tom was experiencing.

It was not Tom's fault that he was a burnout, and he was not doing it purposefully to make women suffer. Most likely, the roots of his burnout lay in the on-again, off-again nature of his marriage to Sara, or maybe it was being left for another man. Regardless of the cause, Tom's personality after his divorce was much different from Joshua's.

When Tom finally began dating again, his relationships quickly took on a pattern. He would meet a woman he was attracted to and pursue her. In fact, the more he had to pursue a woman, the more he wanted her. Many such dates were arranged by friends who had vetted the woman beforehand and could attest to her character. Many were attractive women who, like Tom, had professional careers.

But as soon as Tom began to feel that a woman was attracted to him, he would begin to feel that something was missing. It's not that he became critical of these women. On the contrary, he could sing their praises and recite their assets. When a close friend suggested that Tom was being overly picky about the women he'd been dating, his response was that maybe he was just being "choosy," and that as desirable as each of these women was, none was just the "right one" for him.

A Cautious Man Versus a Burned-Out One

Unlike Maria (in Chapter 1), who let herself believe that true love strikes like lightning and acted impulsively, Joshua and Brigitte both intentionally took their time. Some attraction—call it chemistry—between them was there to begin with, but it deepened and grew more intense over time. Brigitte deserves credit for not thinking there was something lacking in Joshua because he was willing to be friends or that it took some time for him to write that letter. After all, she also was cautious. In the end, I believed that this couple would almost certainly marry, and that Joshua's dream of a happy adulthood might very well come true.

In terms of what I am talking about here, Joshua would most likely be a "keeper." In contrast, any woman would be well advised to think twice about a man whose personality is more like Tom's.

Dating a Cautious Man

If you believe you might be dating a man who is more like Joshua (cautious) than Tom (burned out), here are some things to do:

- Continue spending time with him, but slow down the agenda. Be friends for a while and see what happens.
- Don't be sexually intimate. If you've already crossed this line, try backtracking. Explain that you liked making love, but want to take a step back for a while.
- As you get to know each other better, be honest about some of your earlier experiences in relationships.
- Have fun. Try doing different things together and being together in a variety of different situations.
- When you are comfortable doing so, share your vision about what you have always imagined a satisfying adult life would be.

Chapter Three

Think Carefully Before "Surrendering"

When I talk about *surrender* in relationships, I need to distinguish one form of surrender, which could be called healthy, from one that is highly dysfunctional. Simply put, it's one thing to "surrender" to love—to allow ourselves to flow with passion, as opposed to resisting it, regardless of whether that resistance is the result of caution or burnout. Tom (described in Chapter 2) was an example of someone who would extinguish any passion within him by convincing himself it wasn't enough. Joshua (also in Chapter 2), by contrast, acknowledged his feelings for what they were but chose to keep them to himself. Eventually, he surrendered to his feelings, with a happy result.

Now let's look at the other form of surrender. If a woman believes, even for one second, that she's going to find or keep a good man by intentionally letting him believe he is right and in control all the time, she might as well plug his head into a tire inflator and turn it on. Trying to market yourself to men by communicating that you will defer to them (in the hope that they will then treat you fairly and respectfully) may work in the short run because it may appeal to the egos of some men (especially those who are control freaks), but it is a losing strategy in the long run.

Every responsible father needs to teach his son how to walk this line: to feel competent and self-confident, but not arrogant. The best way to accomplish this is to coach boys to be willing to face challenges and to persevere in the face of adversity. At the same time, it is important to teach

Self-Esteem Versus Omnipotence

In order to maintain healthy self-esteem, men need to feel a sense of empowerment and competence, but they do not need to feel omnipotent. Believing you are totally in control quickly leads to believing you can make no mistakes, which is fatal to a relationship.

them that it is acceptable to have limitations, and that they are neither infallible nor bullet-proof.

In other words, to be mentally healthy, men need to be able to maintain a balance between ego and humility. That is the basis for healthy self-esteem in a man, and it is also the foundation of a good, lasting relationship.

Within some social circles, it is popular to advocate for what are sometimes referred to as "traditional" gender roles for men and women. However, this is often little more than a euphemistic attempt to forward the idea that it is the man's natural or God-given role to lead and to be the decision maker, while it is the woman's natural role to follow and obey without questioning.

Whether she truly believed this or not, one author of a book on relationships advised a woman to consciously work to make the man in her life believe he is in control and right all the time. On reading this book more closely, one gets the impression that the goal is to create an illusion other than reality—to let the man *think* he's in control, while subtly manipulating him to get what you want. It's just a variation on the old saw that a man should never argue with his wife—she's always right.

People laugh at ideas like that and speak about them with a wink. However, there are women who take such advice about their proper place in a relationship seriously and make every effort to be as obsequious as possible. They may even affiliate with a religion that advocates this kind of surrender. Most of these women sooner or later find themselves either exploited to the point of being totally enraged or clinically depressed, or kicked to the curb by the spoiled brat they enabled.

Case Study

Betsy and Brian: The Corruption of Power

Betsy was married to Brian for 20 years. They raised a son and a daughter, he built a successful business, and she finished nursing school by attending class part-time for years. Once both children were in middle school, Betsy increased her job hours from half-time to full-time. Eventually she was promoted to a supervisory position and found, somewhat to her surprise, that she liked it.

Viewed from the outside, Betsy and Brian's marriage (and their family) seemed enviable: a nice house, a good-looking couple, and attractive, talented children. The view from the inside was very different.

Betsy and Brian met when they were attending college—different colleges, in different cities. He was a year ahead of her but knew her from high school, where they shared some friends and ended up at some of the same parties. As boyfriend and girlfriend, though, their time together was pretty much limited to college breaks and summers.

Betsy's parents had divorced when she was eight. She eventually became close to her father and stepmother, but for a long time her life centered around her mother and younger brother, whom she lived with. She described their lifestyle as comfortable but hardly cushy. Betsy was a sweet, responsible child who genuinely enjoyed being helpful, even when it came to helping prepare meals and looking after her brother.

Brian, meanwhile, came from a successful, competitive family of professionals. He was good-looking, social, athletic, and driven—qualities Betsy admired, especially since she tended to be shy. For his part, Brian said it was Betsy's sunny disposition, thoughtfulness, easygoing manner, and good looks that attracted him to her.

After putting it off for nearly two years, Brian and Betsy started having sex the summer between Brian's junior and senior years. In September Betsy discovered she was pregnant, and Brian promptly proposed marriage. Betsy dropped out of college and lived with her mother while Brian finished school. He was on campus when their son was born and was not present for the delivery. That summer he quickly found a job, and with some help from both families, they set up a household.

For Brian and Betsy, who considered themselves spiritual people, religion was an important part of family life. They joined a very conservative religious sect, one that took a "traditional" view of male and female roles. Though privately Betsy felt some discomfort with the idea that her role was to obey while Brian's was to lead, for a long time they did not butt heads over this. If anything, Brian seemed to be a benign leader, and Betsy was comfortable in her own skin, being the kind and loving person she'd always been.

There is an old saying: Power corrupts, and absolute power corrupts absolutely. That, unfortunately, is what happened to Brian. The man who started out as something akin to a benign king of his castle eventually evolved into a self-absorbed despot who insisted on having everything his way and quickly became testy if he encountered resistance. Betsy had to admit that she played a part in facilitating this change, which took place gradually and insidiously.

Brian was not—at least early on in the marriage—a man who had to have his own way all the time, whose first priority was always himself and what he wanted, or who was stingy when it came to money and caring for his family. In time, though, he became all of these things. What was most annoying to Betsy was that over time he developed a habit of asking,

"What's in it for me?" whenever she would ask him for something.

He would also insist that she "earn" any gifts or privileges she got. For instance, when she asked for a pair of diamond stud earrings to commemorate their tenth anniversary, Brian initially dismissed it as a waste of money. "You don't need such extravagances," he declared. Then, later, as if thinking it over, he proposed that they buy Betsy the earrings, but only if he bought a set of golf clubs he'd been eyeing.

When she agreed, he drove her to a store in a shopping mall that had advertised a set of diamond earrings for $75. "They were so small you practically had to use a microscope to see them!" Betsy said with a laugh, looking back on it. "And to think that I settled for that, when he went out and spent a thousand dollars on new golf clubs!" She shook her head. "I'm amazed at how I had myself fooled into thinking that was the way marriage should be."

Don't Surrender!

If you are flirting with the idea of surrender, or contemplating the notion that you will be more attractive to men if you define your role as a woman of obedience, take some time to seriously read the marriage vows used by different religions. Take special note of how they are phrased. Do they include words such as "cherish" and "honor," as well as "obey"? Keep in mind that these are vows: They can be considered broken if there is a breakdown in love and respect, not just obedience. Also keep in mind Betsy's experience and what happened to her when she decided to go along with the idea that a wife should be the one to surrender in a marriage.

In contrast to Betsy's dilemma in opting for a role that, in her heart, made her uncomfortable is the situation in which couples commit to "healthy" marriage vows. Such vows ask couples to commit themselves to mutual respect and to stand together through hard times. They ask couples to honor and cherish one another, and to be equal partners on the journey that lies ahead. In the best of relationships no one is asked to surrender.

Chapter Four

Looking for Love in All the Wrong Places

(and Other Bad Marketing Strategies)

With the possible exception of women who genuinely enjoy going to sporting events for their own pleasure, single women are not likely to find a man by sitting in stadiums or cruising sports bars. But once again, following half-baked advice, countless women are doing this—pursuing a strategy of "being where the men are." Examples of similarly ineffective tactics that single women have been known to try include the following:

- Signing up for golf (or tennis) lessons in the belief that wealthy, attractive men play these sports and are just waiting to be found at golf and tennis clubs.
- Going to Alcoholics Anonymous meetings as a way of meeting sober single men.
- Buying a sports car (or truck) to attract the sports car (or truck) loving man.
- Purchasing a large-screen, flat-panel, high-definition television in order to interest a man in spending some time in her house.
- Investing in season tickets in order to be able to invite men to baseball, football, or basketball games.
- Taking skiing lessons so she can hang out on the slopes, looking great to the single skiers as they fly by.

The sad truth is that such strategies usually fail—you may end up with a man who is into one or another of these things much more than he is into you. The crucial thing to consider is whether any of these activities appeals to *you*. On the one hand, if the idea of driving a sports car appeals to you, then by all means consider buying one. If you are in recovery, then

AA meetings are where you belong. And if you enjoy playing golf, it makes sense to develop your skills in that sport.

On the other hand, if you are pursuing one or more such strategy for marketing purposes—in the hope of encountering and attracting single men—chances are you will attract men who aren't really a great fit for you (and vice versa).

Janet signed up for a course with Toastmasters, an organization for people who want to become more proficient and comfortable with public speaking. She also joined two outdoor adventure clubs and signed up for activities ranging from bird-watching to cross-country skiing to a week-long raft trip down the Colorado River. She did these things not because she believed she would encounter single men, but rather because she had always been interested in the activities. Unfortunately, for many years, her life had been taken up with work and part-time school, and Janet had neither the time nor the money to pursue such interests.

Janet and her future husband met on a bird-watching outing on a salt flat at a national seashore on the Massachusetts coast. He was there for the same reasons—pursuing interests he'd long put on hold, one of which turned out to be nature photography.

Please Yourself

A winning strategy for finding compatible men is to think about activities, interests, and skills you either have tried or would like to explore, and then pursue them. Your own genuine interest will be obvious, and this in itself will be attractive to men who share your passion.

Smiling All the Time is Bad For Your Face

There is probably no more ridiculous—yet common—piece of advice offered to women seeking men than the idea that they should be "perky" all the time. Naturally, you don't want to go looking for Mr. Right when you're feeling emotionally drained or totally depressed. I wouldn't advise men to do that, either. For obvious reasons, meeting someone when you're depressed can have a negative outcome.

However, what would you think, and how would you feel, if you were dating a man who smiled all the time and acted as if he never had a bad day in his life? Sound unappealing? Yet this is precisely how women are advised to act. It goes without saying that most people respond positively to a friendly smile. But let's not forget the importance of being sincere. Making sure a house sparkles all the time might be a good strategy for selling it, but making yourself sparkle all the time isn't necessarily a good strategy for finding a good relationship.

Naturally, men appreciate a woman who has a sense of humor, especially if it is similar to their own. Be it silly or sarcastic, erudite or slapstick, a sense of humor is an essential tool for survival. Take it as a good sign if you and the man you are dating find yourselves laughing at the same jokes or find the same movies funny. But don't try to talk yourself into smiling all the time. You'll just end up with wrinkles.

When you're on a date, the idea is to be in a good mood and have a good time. At the same time, you're much better off showing some true emotions, including what makes you happy and sad, joyful and angry. That accomplishes two things. First, it allows you to see how your date likes a real woman. Second, it allows the man you are with to open up to you in return.

There's No Such Place as Stepford, Connecticut!

If you've never seen the film *The Stepford Wives* (either version), rent it immediately. It is hard to keep from laughing (at least it is for me and many people I know) at those ridiculous women from the mythical town of Stepford, Connecticut, always happy and forever compliant with whatever their man wants. Imagine what a man would think of you after a few dates if you acted like that. How would you feel about being in a relationship with a "Stepford man?"

The Motivation Behind Cosmetic Surgery

There is no way that a man writing a book for women about relationships is going to be able to convince his readers that they should never consider cosmetic surgery. That would be like me trying to tell you that you should never buy a diet book. It doesn't matter that research shows that diets tend to be fads that don't work in the long run. The facts notwithstanding, women will still buy diet books, just as they will still consider cosmetic surgery.

A woman once told me that her fiancé confided in her that the one issue he had with what he otherwise saw as a perfect woman was that her breasts were "on the small side." You can fill in the rest of the story for yourself. The woman had implant surgery—nothing too dramatic, but noticeable, nonetheless. Two months later, she came home early from work with a migraine and found you-know-who in bed with a woman who appeared to be sporting D cups. She later discovered that she was engaged to a narcissist who had once coaxed another fiancé into getting implants, just for him.

There is no getting around the reality that our society is obsessed with women's (and men's) appearance. That's why more and more men are having their hair dyed in order to look younger—something only women once did. And cosmetic surgery has its place. For instance, having the lines removed from around your eyes or the wrinkles on your forehead smoothed out in order to avoid being stigmatized as old is becoming more common. Such changes can make you look better, and they may make you feel better about yourself.

Cosmetic breast surgery, by contrast, is something worth mulling over for a long time. If you are looking for a good man and really believe your breasts are the key to finding and keeping Mr. Right, your thinking may reflect the *marketing* approach that has left so many women ultimately unsatisfied.

If You Do it, Do it for You, and Only You

Once again, the rule to keep in mind is this: Who are you doing it for? If surgery to remove the lines beneath your eyes will make you feel better about yourself, that's one thing. But if it's just something that your boyfriend thinks you should do, you owe it to yourself to think twice.

Chapter Five

To Shrink or Not to Shrink

In the movie *Annie Hall,* Woody Allen and Diane Keaton are trying to work out their relationship with the help of their respective therapists. It's a scream to watch each of them tell his or her side of the evolving story. It's a tongue-in-cheek view of therapy, with the therapists tending to be sympathetic to whichever side of the story they are hearing. Allen's character is seeking sex, while Keaton's character talks about the potential for a relationship. He wants to go to bed now and talk later; she wants to talk first. Clearly, Allen is poking fun at the conflicting stereotypes about what men and women really want.

Avoid Therapy as a Marketing Strategy

Many advice books for women either suggest or state outright that a woman's only hope of finding a relationship is to begin by "cleaning house" through personal therapy. "You can't have a good relationship with someone," this advice goes, "unless you feel good about yourself first."

So, women who choose to follow this advice seek out the therapist who will help them identify and "work through" their issues in the hope that this psychological cleansing will make them more appealing and capable of finding and keeping a good man. It's sort of a psychological marketing strategy.

I have nothing against personal therapy, for men or women. I am a psychologist, after all. In the examples given in earlier chapters, you could argue that both Karen and Sara might have benefited from therapy, and that counseling might even have saved their marriages. It's also possible that neither of these women believed they had issues worth delving into.

As helpful as therapy can be, using therapy as a marketing strategy strikes me as just another dead end. It won't give you some kind of "certificate of mental health" that makes you more attractive to men.

The idea that you can't find happiness in a relationship without first finding happiness by yourself—or its variation, that personal therapy will pave the way to happiness—is actually a new idea, historically. Not so long ago, the prevailing wisdom was just the opposite—that it was only through a relationship that a person could realize his or her full potential and achieve fulfillment. In times past, a good relationship was thought to be the key to mental health, not vice versa.

In describing his relationship with his wife, French writer Alexis de Tocqueville gave this account of married life as it was for him in the nineteenth century: "I cannot describe to you the happiness yielded in the long run by the habitual society of a woman, in whose soul all that is good in your own is reflected naturally, and even improved."

Look For Your Best Self in a Relationship

Flowery as it may be, that quote succinctly captures the idea that a good relationship can bring out the best in us. Generations past had little

Will Therapy Make You More Attractive?

What about the idea of personal therapy? Is it a good idea for you? If you are trying to decide whether you should seek therapy, the following guidelines might help:

- If, after reading Part Two of this book, you conclude that you have made the mistake of committing yourself to one or more of the types of men described (or to the same type more than once), therapy might be helpful—if you make its goal the development of an ability to more honestly assess the men you meet and are willing to do so. Chances are, you are making commitment mistakes because you are not being honest with yourself when it comes to taking the measure of the men you meet. Or you may be focusing too much on marketing yourself and not enough on being selective.
- If you see more than a little of yourself in one of the descriptions of men in Part Two, therapy may also be appropriate. As the examples of Karen and Sara show, men do not hold a monopoly on insecurity or narcissism. Any such tendencies on your part can just as easily sabotage a relationship.

If neither of the above describes you (at least as you are right now) chances are you're just fine and should not consider therapy as something that will help you find a man worth keeping.

argument with the concept that personal fulfillment was most likely to be achieved through marriage. Many people today, however, are inclined to look on this idea cynically, preferring to believe that each of us needs to create our own happiness and not have any such expectations for a relationship. That belief may simply reflect the disappointments and frustrations that so many people have endured.

The social reality today is much different than it was a hundred years ago. Back then, divorce was rare, and few people remained single. Novels like *Anna Karenina* by Leo Tolstoy and *Ethan Frome* by Edith Wharton were moral tales that foretold the dire consequences of infidelity and divorce. Today, the easing of the taboo that once kept divorce rates low has resulted in an entire culture of single men and women. In that kind of environment, where finding a good partner is far from assured, it may make sense to believe that you need to find peace with yourself and be able to carve out a fulfilling life on your own.

Still, there may be more than a kernel of truth in the idea that, as happy as we may be, a good relationship can help us realize our full potential and bring out our best qualities. I believe that this hope remains alive in the hearts of many men and women.

Finding a Good Man: The Selective Approach

Part Two gets down to the task of identifying and understanding the most common mistakes women make when trying to decide if a man is a good candidate for a relationship. Here you will find descriptions of six different types of "problem men."

Part Two is also a primer of sorts on male development, in that it includes explanations of how upbringing influences personality development, presented in nontechnical terms and illustrated with cogent examples.

No doubt you will recognize the personalities described here, as well as elements of the various personality "inventories" included in these chapters, in some of the men you have known. Beyond that, you will come to appreciate just how deeply rooted these character types can be and why it is a mistake to believe that love alone will change their most extreme manifestations.

No one is perfect, and almost everyone has at least some degree of a few of the qualities described in these chapters. Depending on just how severe a man's problem personality may be, though, you may need to think about letting go and moving on, rather than trying to deal with it. If you are already in a relationship with such a man, that decision can be difficult to make. You need to decide between cutting your losses and committing even more of your precious time and energy. Hopefully, the material in Part Two and Part Three will help you with such deliberations.

When some women hear the word *selective* used in a discussion of dating, they react by saying their problem is finding men. To them, the idea of being selective makes this process even more difficult. In truth, the selective approach (versus the marketing approach described earlier) is actually more likely to prove to be the winning strategy.

The selective approach increases your chances of finding a good relationship for two reasons:

1. By following the selective approach, you use your valuable time more efficiently. How much time have you wasted pursuing a relationship that you later realized was not really worth the effort? How much time would you have saved by thoughtfully assessing the chances that this relationship would last?

2. The selective approach not only helps you identify relationships that are not worth pursuing, it also helps you identify men who, while not perfect, have the potential to be good partners.

With these two thoughts in mind, let's look at some different types of men. You probably won't be able to tell if a man you are attracted to has one of the problem personalities described here the first time you meet him. However, as you spend time together, being aware of the signs described in the following chapters will put you in a position to start using the selective approach. Most likely, you'll start getting a gut feeling, one way or the other.

Then comes the critical test: Will you trust that gut feeling and look a little more carefully, or will you put your blinders on and ignore what your gut tells you?

Chapter Six

Problem Man #1
Mr. Insecurity

Boys have long been thought to be inherently tough and rugged, almost to the point of insensitivity. This is probably the main reason so many boys have historically been the objects of abuse and neglect. Bullying, for example, has long been common among boys, and for a long time not much thought was given to it. Boys were expected to deal with bullying themselves, by fighting back. Boys, in turn, typically internalized these societal attitudes. Even today, most boys are not disposed to "snitch" on a bully. Similarly, as headlines over the past few years can attest, sexual abuse of boys has long been under-reported. Significantly, this widespread but largely hidden abuse that boys have had to endure may help to explain why insecurity—the topic of this chapter—is so prevalent among men.

Stereotypes about boys notwithstanding, research has shown that boys are, in fact, very sensitive to abuse, neglect, or abandonment. Of course, there are degrees of neglect and abuse. Depending on how severe early abuse is—combined with a given individual's capacity for resilience—its effects on a man's adult personality can be more or less severe.

In general, boys who are born with inherently sensitive temperaments—and mothers can usually identify such sensitive boys from a very early age—suffer more severe effects from abuse or neglect. In a word, they become *insecure*. One such man, looking back on a hard childhood, identified himself as sensitive by nature. His way of coping with a harsh family life was to pretend he was a leprechaun and could disappear at will. In reality, whenever he sensed the level of tension in the house rising to the point where someone might get hit, he would "disappear" into his bedroom or into his tree house.

Parents who are inclined to be neglectful, who discipline very severely, or who hold back affection, approval, and even physical comforts (ironically, sometimes in a misguided effort to make a boy tougher) are likely to sow the seeds of insecurity even in a boy who is not necessarily very sensitive. They will certainly do so in one who is. At the same time, such a parenting style will instill a sense of *underentitlement*—the feeling that he is not very important or deserving.

Get Him to Tell His Story

It usually isn't difficult to gain some insight into a man's upbringing and deduce whether it should be described as nurturing and supportive or harsh and abusive. Just express some interest in knowing about his family and a man will most likely be happy to talk about himself. Keep an ear open for the following:

- People who have had harsh childhoods and suffered abuse or neglect may understandably be reluctant to talk about it. In fact, a reluctance to talk about the past at all can be a tip-off that abuse or neglect may have been an issue in a man's upbringing.
- Ask about family traditions such as holidays and birthdays. Does he seem to have happy memories of these events? If so, take that as a positive sign. If not, try asking a couple of questions about why holidays were not something he looked forward to.
- Ask him to give you a "snapshot" description of his mother and father, and see how he describes them.

The Insecure Man is a Complex Man

The insecure man can present a complex picture, parts of which can be quite alluring. He is a man who is apt to be highly critical of others and demanding of himself, while describing himself as someone who simply has high standards. This can be appealing to some women, especially those who feel that the last man they were involved with was lazy or sloppy. However, in indulging his critical nature, the insecure man is re-creating in his adult life the rejecting environment he grew up in. You can think of his behavior as a reflection of his pervasive feelings of underentitlement— that no one is living up to expectations, including himself, and that therefore no one is deserving of rewards or praise. Sooner or later, you can expect him to apply this philosophy to you.

The insecure man is fundamentally distrustful. And no wonder: As a child, he could not count on love, nurturance, or even protection. The more severe the abuse or neglect, the deeper his distrust. As an adult, such a man might see himself not as distrustful, but rather as someone who takes pride in not being naive or gullible. He just sees himself as someone who looks at others through a lens of healthy skepticism. He's forever vigilant against being taken advantage of or lied to. To a woman who feels that she, too, has been taken advantage of in the past as a result of being overly trusting or naive, such qualities in a man can have considerable appeal. It's akin to having something in common.

The insecure man can also come across as strong or tough, and again, this can be appealing. Beneath that tough exterior, however, the insecure man is withholding and needy. He is stingy with love and attention (often with money as well), while demanding it from you or others. If you fall for this false strongman image of an insecure man, you will soon find yourself in a relationship where no matter what you do or how hard you try, it is never enough to satisfy this man. Viewed from his perspective, you are always falling short, always letting him down. The worst thing you can do is buy into that idea.

The Importance of Establishing Limits

If you are not careful to establish limits on what you are (and are not) willing to give in a relationship with an insecure man, you may quickly find yourself becoming the object of abuse as punishment for, from his point of view, your failures or inadequacies. You will most definitely feel drained by the insecure man's unquenchable thirst for attention and approval. In your relationship with Mr. Insecurity, look for him to feel easily abandoned (by you), and to experience discomfort and be overly self-conscious in most social situations.

Many insecure men never realize the potential they have, but instead live the life of an underachiever. They may fall victim to self-pity, as though life has let them down. There is a kernel of truth in this perception, in that they did not receive the love, support, and nurturance they needed early on, when they were most vulnerable. These insecure men will be easy to spot, because of their pattern of never doing as well as they can and never achieving what they are capable of. Often they will quit rather than persevere in the face of adversity.

Other insecure men can be very successful, particularly in terms of their careers. Their insecurity can be much harder to identify, at least initially. Usually, these men come from families in which any abuse or neglect that occurred was psychological rather than physical. They often had fathers who were models of success but who were also critical and emotionally distant. Blessed with intelligence and talent, these boys compensate and often go on to become men who are hard-working and driven. Through their efforts they win approval and attention, which becomes a goal in and of itself. The woman in a relationship with this kind of insecure man may say that he is well respected by colleagues or thought of as a success by the community, and he may do a lot of things to create and maintain that image. But in his most personal relationships, signs of insecurity will emerge.

Love Alone Does Not Heal All Wounds

If you begin to suspect that the man you are attracted to (or are getting involved with) is fairly insecure, be aware that no matter how he may wish to come across to others, inwardly he feels empty. He's looking for someone to fill a deep sense of emptiness and anxiety. And—watch out!—he's also looking for someone to vent his anger on.

If the insecure man is at least able to recognize how his past has affected him and has made some efforts to rise above it (perhaps through counseling), and if he is not *severely* insecure, then you might consider pursuing the relationship further.

Above all, though, you should avoid trying to convince yourself that love alone will change him. Grace is a woman who made this mistake.

Case Study

Grace and Adam: A Need to Connect the Dots

When she first met Adam, Grace thought that he was just shy and quiet. She had no idea that what she was seeing was severe insecurity. He was one type of insecure man—the underachiever. Though he had graduated from college and was employed as an engineer, Adam had never advanced very far. He usually got evaluations that boiled down to "meets expectations"—in other words, good but far short of what was needed to get ahead.

Once Grace committed to the relationship—which she did mainly because Adam, unlike her previous two boyfriends, had a steady job and was faithful to her—things got steadily worse for her. Adam was constantly finding fault with her, from the way she cooked and cleaned to the way she spoke and the opinions she expressed. At first, his criticism took the form of sarcasm; as time went on, however, he would become explosively angry, shouting, throwing things, and calling her crude, demeaning names. To make matters worse, the more she tried to live up to his standards in order to avoid making him angry, the less it seemed to take to get him to the point where he would explode.

Three years later, after Adam was arrested for assaulting Grace, she finally came to the conclusion that they must divorce. Naturally, she was both hurt and confused. She also felt that she had allowed Adam to humiliate her, which deeply hurt her self-respect. She felt guilty—she couldn't help but wonder if she'd somehow created a monster.

Grace had unwittingly let herself become hopelessly entangled in Adam's insecurity and the distorted perceptions it created. It wasn't as if she wanted to bring out the worst in this insecure man. On the contrary, her sole motivation had been to try to keep the peace. But as with jealousy, once insecurity rears its head, the worst thing a person can do is feed it. That's what Grace had unintentionally done.

Grace knew that her marriage to Adam was over, but for a long time she struggled with the idea of how much of it was his fault and how much was hers. Had she simply made a bad choice by not recognizing Adam's severe insecurity from the start? Had she, despite her good intentions, actually played into and fed Adam's insecurity? Or had she—as Adam claimed—actually *made* him insecure and full of rage?

My message is simple: You cannot make a man insecure if he isn't insecure to begin with. Keep in mind that his insecurity has its roots in his childhood, not in his relationship with you. The only mistake you can make is the mistake that Grace innocently made, which was to feed the demon once it showed itself. She did this because she believed that she could heal Adam simply by loving him, without him ever having to acknowledge his insecurity or take responsibility for how it affected him.

Look for Some Insight

The chances of an insecure man rising above his insecurity and having a relationship that is based on mutual respect and love—as opposed to neediness—totally depends on his ability to recognize his insecurity. He may not call it that, but he must be able to take responsibility for its symptoms, such as the insatiable need for attention and reassurance, the irrational jealousy, and the distrust. If he sees his neediness as the result of others' failures to do right by him, or his jealousy as something that you are creating, chances are he will remain insecure. The best course is to avoid such men, as they are just going to soak up all your time and energy and leave you feeling like a failure.

Despite his growing criticism, his smothering manner, and his increasing anger, Grace persisted in believing that if she just loved Adam enough, he would come to believe in her love and things would then get better. Instead, things went steadily downhill.

Early signs of Adam's insecurity were easy to see, although Grace, like many women, did not recognize them for what they were. Because she did not understand insecurity or how it operates in relationships, she could not "connect the dots" and understand the situation. So, like many women, she just hung in there, tried her hardest to be a good partner, and hoped things would get better.

Recognize Insecurity

The signs of insecurity include those already mentioned, plus these:

Being Thin-Skinned

One of the first things Grace noticed about Adam was how easily his feelings were hurt. Often, she did not realize that he was feeling hurt until she saw it in his face. Then she had to figure out why, which also wasn't easy. His typical pattern was to withdraw and sulk, and get angry later on. Adam could feel hurt by something as simple as feeling ignored by Grace. He could also be upset by relying on his idea that if she loved him, she should know how he was feeling or what he wanted, without having to tell her.

Needing Constant Reassurance and Approval

Another thing Grace knew about Adam was that he was easily deflated. He was quick to make self-deprecating remarks like, "That was pretty stupid," or even, "What a loser!" Grace sometimes responded to such comments by pointing out to Adam that he had a college degree and a good job, or just saying that it wasn't true.

Smothering

Once Grace got hooked into a relationship with Adam, he quickly became more or less glued to her at the hip. He wanted them to be together all the time. He didn't even like it when she was in a different room in the apartment they shared, and would come and sit beside her.

Being Jealous

No one would describe Grace as a social butterfly; however, she did have friends and was close to her family. It wasn't long before Adam began—in little ways at first—to question Grace when she wanted to spend time with friends or family. In time, this became a major sore point between them, to the degree that, when Grace was out with a friend or paying a visit to her sister, Adam would call her on her cell phone three or four times. And if friends or family would call when Grace was not at home, Adam would often "forget" to give her the message.

Distrusting Others

As an insecure man, Adam was not only jealous of Grace's other relationships, but also distrustful of others in general. He was forever suspicious of others' motives, believing that people wanted to take advantage of him. As a result, he was very critical of others, quick to find fault and point out flaws. Grace found this especially annoying when Adam criticized her family or friends or questioned their motives, when she knew very well that these people loved and cared about her.

Don't be Tempted by an Insecure Man

Hopefully, armed with knowledge of the signs and symptoms of insecurity, you will be able to connect the dots in a way that Grace could not. It's really not so surprising that many women, like Grace, fail to see insecurity for what it is—at least not until they're already well into a relationship with an insecure man. Often, it isn't until a commitment has been made that insecurity presents itself in full view. At that point, as many women can attest, you may begin to feel that you are living in an emotional prison.

Insecure men like Adam can (and usually do) partially control or disguise their insecurity at first, because they are instinctively ashamed of it and know that it isn't attractive. Also, they tend not to see themselves as insecure, but rather as shy or having high standards, or sometimes as misunderstood victims. Self-pity is common among insecure men. Meanwhile, women who are attracted to such men may minimize the insecurity that is staring them in the face and instead see a man who merely needs a little

What You See Is What You Get

If you think your love will be enough to cure a man's insecurity, don't bet on it. Instead of telling yourself that love heals all wounds, try this reality: What you see is what you get. In fact, if you fail to recognize insecurity for what it is and think you can heal it just by loving him enough, the situation is likely to get worse, not better.

her. Ling had been the oldest of five children. Her mother's emotional problems took the form of frequent retreats to her bedroom, where she would lock herself in, complaining of a supposed headache, and not come out for hours. While she was locked away, the kids were left to fend for themselves. Ling believed her excuse about the headaches for a long time. But by the time she was a teenager, Ling knew, from her mother's behavior and seeing prescription bottles in the medicine cabinet, that it was depression, not headaches, that kept her bedridden.

Because of her mother's frequent absences, from the time she was six or seven Ling had progressively taken on more and more responsibility for her younger siblings. Meanwhile, despite her daughter's best efforts, Ling's mother would always manage to find fault with what she'd done. Usually, she'd imply that Ling's efforts were a poor substitute for what she could do herself, if it weren't for her headaches. This kind of constant criticism (think of it as a form of abuse) can produce insecurity in both boys and girls.

Although Jack did not use that term himself, he described Ling as manifesting many of the symptoms of insecurity described in this chapter. She was thin-skinned, easily hurt, and easily defeated. Jake could never predict when she would take offense at something he said and was often caught off guard by her reaction to some seemingly innocuous comment from him or someone else. Sometimes she would say that she was hurt because he wasn't paying enough attention to her. And she could not be teased at all.

If Jake went out to a local sports bar, as he sometimes did with a small group of male friends who had maintained contact after graduating, Ling would call him six or seven times on his cell phone. At home, she would routinely check his e-mail on their computer and peruse his cell phone log. If they were out somewhere, she would usually accuse him of looking at other women. In many ways, she was a female version of Adam, described earlier in the chapter.

Jake admitted that he was apt to cast a glance at attractive women, especially those who obviously wanted to be noticed. But he denied that he was a flirt, claimed that his interest went no further than looking, and insisted that he had never cheated on Ling.

Jake was already an experienced caretaker when he met Ling. In other words, you could say that he was already primed to get into a relationship with someone who was needy and insecure. This seems to be true as well for many women who get involved with insecure men: They are already experienced caretakers *before* they meet these men.

Your Capacity to Nurture Can Make You Vulnerable

Basically, what Jake did when he met Ling was to use taking care of her as a substitute for taking care of his mother. In a way, marrying Ling was his ticket out of his mother's house. He admitted that he was drawn to Ling, in part because she needed him, and that at the time he was beginning to feel trapped by his mother's dependency. In effect, he went from mothering his mother to mothering his wife.

Unfortunately, despite all of Jake's efforts, after six years of marriage and two children, Ling was still a financial and emotional mess. Loving Ling and taking care of her did not solve her problems; nor did it make her insecurity go away. On the contrary, both only got worse. She still could not manage money, was prone to depression, and seemed incapable of handling the complex responsibilities that life demands of couples today,

Don't Blame Mom!

Who is to blame for making people insecure? The common belief is that insecurity is the result of some failure of mothering. In truth, though, fathers can be just as responsible for generating insecurity, especially in boys. If you find yourself interested in a man, ask him some questions not just about his relationship with his mother and what kind of person she was or is, but also about how he feels about his father and their relationship when he was growing up. To grow up secure, boys need not only nurturance, but also support and an effective role model whom they can respect and emulate. Fathers can nurture just as mothers can.

Secure men typically report having had fairly good relationships with their fathers and feel good about their fathers now. If the man you are checking out responds this way, take it as a good sign. However, if he avoids talking about his father, seems uncomfortable being asked about his relationship with him, has no relationship with him, or frankly describes the relationship as bad or abusive, watch out! He is probably insecure. The question is, *how* insecure?

Meanwhile, keep this important point in mind: Chances are, it was not solely a man's mother's fault that he is insecure, and it is not likely that you will cure his insecurity just by slipping into a maternal role with him.

such as raising children, keeping up a household, and maybe even holding down a job, all at the same time. So Jake found himself having to do this mostly on his own. He was continually having to dig the family out of debt, as well as doing most of the work around the house. Ling worked on and off, but always part-time, and never long enough to allow them to rely on her income and figure it into their budget.

Even though you are a woman, maybe you can identify with Jake. Maybe you are drawn to men who are the male equivalent of Ling. What you need to understand is that, like Jake, your capacity to nurture is both a personal asset and a personal vulnerability. With the right man—meaning a man who is also capable of nurturing—this can be a good thing. You can look after each other, share the workload of life, and perhaps even bring out the best in each other, in the way that de Tocqueville described his marriage (see Chapter 5). On the other hand, with an insecure man, life will likely become a one-way street, as it was for Jake.

Measuring Insecurity: The Insecurity Inventory

By now, you might be wondering if the man you're dating (or thinking about dating) is insecure. If you suspect he is, you might wonder if you should just walk away now, while you still easily can.

You may have noticed some signs of insecurity. That's okay. The challenge you face is to determine just how severe the insecurity is. Is it so bad that it will probably wreck any relationship you may try to establish? Or is it not all that severe? After all, few (if any) people can be described as totally secure, so what I am talking about here is a matter of degree.

The purpose of the Insecurity Inventory that follows is to help you answer these questions. The inventory is based on the notion that insecurity is not an all-or-nothing quality, something a person (male or female) either has or doesn't have. Rather, insecurity can vary from mild to severe. I included the case of Adam because it is an extreme example showing how a high level of insecurity can kill a relationship.

It is possible for moderate insecurity to be healed, but only if that healing starts with a man acknowledging his insecurity. If he does that, it follows that all the symptoms of insecurity—the smothering, the distrust—become his responsibility, not yours. That's the only starting point for overcoming insecurity that makes any sense. Even then, the guidance of a skilled therapist can be of great help.

The following inventory yields an Insecurity Index that can give you an idea of just how insecure a man is. You can also use the index as a tool to honestly evaluate yourself for signs of insecurity. The less severe the insecurity, the less dangerous it is to a relationship, and the more likely that it can be overcome. However, the starting point remains the same—recognizing insecurity for what it is and how it affects you.

Instructions

Each of the following statements describes a personality trait. Rate the man you are interested in as it describes him, from 0 (not at all) to 10 (totally). After you finish, add up your ratings for an Insecurity Index.

1. Prefers routine; does not like to be spontaneous. 0 1 2 3 4 5 6 7 8 9 10
2. Does not like to take risks. 0 1 2 3 4 5 6 7 8 9 10
3. Distrusts other people in general. 0 1 2 3 4 5 6 7 8 9 10
4. Is thin-skinned (easily offended). 0 1 2 3 4 5 6 7 8 9 10
5. Is self-conscious. 0 1 2 3 4 5 6 7 8 9 10
6. Feels abandoned easily. 0 1 2 3 4 5 6 7 8 9 10
7. Is jealous of your friends and other relationships. 0 1 2 3 4 5 6 7 8 9 10
8. Feels easily defeated. 0 1 2 3 4 5 6 7 8 9 10
9. Blames you for making him angry or jealous. 0 1 2 3 4 5 6 7 8 9 10
10. Is uncomfortable in most social situations. 0 1 2 3 4 5 6 7 8 9 10

Insecurity Index: ____

You're not likely to meet many men with Insecurity Indexes of 0 or 100. If your honest assessment, though, is that you are in a relationship with a man who has an Insecurity Index higher than 50, you need to take notice.

What Do I Do Now?

After reading this chapter and applying the Insecurity Inventory to a man you are interested in, you should have some idea whether insecurity is an issue you are facing and how severe it is. Let's say it looks as if you are faced with some moderate insecurity. What should you do next?

Part Three of this book describes four critical tests you can use to decide if the relationship has enough potential to warrant your valuable time and effort. I suggest you read that Part and apply those tests before going further in the relationship. An insecure man who passes all of those tests is definitely more likely to be a keeper than one who fails all or most of them.

Part Four includes practical advice for coping with a man who has a problem personality of one kind or another. One of these is the insecure man. Again, since none of us is perfect, most people conclude that it is better to try to work with a mild to moderate problem and to try to overcome it than to either look for a perfect partner or to simply walk away. This is especially true if a man passes all the critical tests in Part Three.

However, if the insecurity you are facing is rather severe (an Insecurity Index of 75 or higher), and if the man you are seeing fails two or more of the critical tests in Part Three, then you need to face the fact that this man will become increasingly difficult for you to live with. The one hope you have is that he will at some point recognize his insecurity and show some real determination (not just talk) to overcome it.

Hopefully, even a moderately insecure man will be able to at least take this first step and acknowledge his insecurity. If you think it would not backfire, you might consider sharing the impression you got from the Insecurity Inventory, though you may want to simply point out some of the behaviors you've observed, rather than giving him his actual Insecurity Index, which may come across as overly clinical. This strategy is most likely to be helpful with a man who is not severely insecure (an Insecurity Index of 50 or less), since this kind of man is less likely to be defensive than the severely insecure man—less likely to accuse you, for instance, of trying to make him out to be "mentally ill." In contrast, you can expect the very insecure man to become angry and defensive when confronted with even the idea that he is insecure. In such a case, it can be better to deal with the problem in the context of therapy.

Regardless of how insecure a man may be, there might come a time when you feel you have no choice but to face up to the problem and name insecurity for what it is. If you believe that insecurity is the main issue facing you in your relationship now, and after going through the critical tests described in Part Three, you may want to skip to Part Four and read Chapter 16 on living with an insecure man, to get some concrete advice about how to proceed.

Or you can continue reading in this Part and educate yourself about the various other kinds of problem men you may encounter and how to identify and evaluate the prospects for having a good relationship with one of them.

Chapter Seven

Problem Man #2
The Narcissist

In Greek mythology, Narcissus was a young man renowned for his beauty. In one version of the myth, Narcissus is lured into a wooded area. There, he discovers a still pool, kneels down beside it, gazes into the water, and immediately falls in love with the overwhelmingly beautiful image he sees before him. When he bends down to kiss this beauty, he discovers that it is his own reflection. Overcome with despair, Narcissus throws himself into the pool and drowns.

If we apply the myth of Narcissus to the kind of man I will describe here, we can sum it up in one simple phrase: It's all about him.

Raising a Narcissist

Finding a good man is about being able to both spot and avoid the bad ones, and this chapter identifies a second potential mistake of huge importance. Just as abuse and neglect can vary greatly in intensity and lead to insecurity, so can coddling vary from mild to severe and lead to an inflated sense of importance—in other words, narcissism.

When I talk about a narcissist, I am talking about a man who was raised in a particular way.

He Coped With Only Lax Limits

Typically, he could do pretty much what he wanted to do. He seldom heard the word no and was able to talk his parents into giving him his way with little difficulty. He may not have had a father in the home, or perhaps his father was largely absent from his life. As a result of this combination of poor limits and an ability to schmooze to get his way, he can be superficially charming, at least as long as things go his way.

He Was Indulged

He got pretty much whatever he wanted and was rarely denied gratification. As a result, he is very much in touch with his feelings and desires, and is able to articulate them. This may make him look like a sensitive or insightful person, but in fact, he's sensitive and insightful only when it comes to getting what he wants.

Expectations of Him Were Low

He did not have many expectations placed on him for responsibility or achievement. Whatever he did was good enough, and he was not expected to work in order to earn rewards. The result is that when faced with frustration or adversity, he typically gives up or changes direction, rather than persevering.

He Was Made to Feel Overentitled

He was generally treated as though he was the center of the universe—someone who could do no wrong and did not deserve to be denied whatever he wanted. So it's little wonder that, as an adult, "it's all about him."

As a consequence of these elements of parenting, a boy grows into a man who holds unrealistic and inflated expectations about what he is entitled to. Because life as a boy was easy for him, he believes it should be that way in adulthood as well. He also believes that others should treat him as if he were special and should go out of their way to make sure he is happy. He doesn't go out of his way to make others unhappy; the bottom line is that his happiness is more important than their happiness.

As is true for abuse and the insecurity it creates, coddling can vary from mild to severe and will be reflected in the degree to which a man is narcissistic.

Women need to be able to identify two types of narcissistic men: the underachiever and the gifted narcissist. After that, it's a matter of determining just how narcissistic a man is and whether pursuing a relationship with him will be worth your time and energy. The insights you gain from the discussion in this chapter should help you make that decision.

Spotting the Underachiever

The most prevalent type of narcissist is the underachiever. Most spoiled boys grow into men who are narcissistic and chronic underachievers. Insecure men can also be underachievers, but for different reasons.

The insecure man is *underentitled*. In his heart, he does not believe he is very capable or deserving of much from life. He expects to be denied and to fail. That is why he is likely to be an underachiever who never realizes his full potential, whatever that may be in terms of innate talents and abilities.

The narcissistic man is also not likely to realize his potential, but for a different reason: He grew up believing that he shouldn't have to work hard for anything or persevere in the face of adversity. In a word, he is *overentitled* and expects the world to beat a path to his doorway.

I once worked with this type of narcissist, a man who fancied himself a great inventor. He would come up with ideas, none of which he would pursue with any degree of effort or perseverance. The result was that all of his great ideas remained in various stages of completion, with no finished products to show for his efforts. At some later point, however, if this man would read about someone who did follow through and actually produced something similar to his idea, he'd express genuine resentment. "That was my idea!" he'd say, as if someone had stolen something that was rightfully his.

Case Study

Kate and Michael: Living with a Free Spirit

One woman committed herself to an underachieving narcissist, much to her eventual dismay. Kate, age 35, had worked as an operating room nurse for 10 years. In order to be successful in this job a person has to be very organized and reliable, as well as able to think quickly on her feet. At the hospital where she worked, Kate was widely regarded as one of the very best. Several surgeons insisted on having her assigned to their cases.

Kate met Michael through friends. She described him as an extremely good-looking man. Kate herself was very attractive, with thick, red, wavy hair, green eyes, and a beautiful complexion. She had been married once and had a daughter, Marcella, who was 10. Her ex-husband was a man she described as also very handsome. "I guess I've always been a sucker for a pretty face," she said with a wry laugh.

In addition to being handsome, Kate's ex was an addict whom she had supported both emotionally and financially. He ended up rewarding Kate for her efforts by cheating on her. Fortunately for Kate, he had not asked for very much in the divorce proceeding (nor was he entitled to much). Kate, a good money manager, had been paying the mortgage and almost all the living expenses during their life together, so she was able to keep the house and maintain her lifestyle after the divorce.

When she looked back on her relationship with Michael, Kate described him as someone who had "all the right moves." At first, Kate pretty much bought the package that Michael was selling. He was a good salesman. He struck her as someone who was sensitive, caring, and funny. He seemed to be in touch with his feelings. He was also a "free spirit" who liked taking long motorcycle rides on Sunday afternoons and who had a wide circle of friends.

Kate recalled that she found these qualities in Michael very attractive, especially since she'd always thought of herself as someone who spent too much time with her nose to the grindstone. Michael, in contrast, seemed spontaneous and fun-loving—two qualities she wanted to have more of. And, perhaps most important, Michael was not an alcoholic or a drug addict.

Kate knew that, in contrast to her, Michael had held many jobs. For the past year, he had been working for a friend doing masonry. But he had plans, he said, to start his own masonry business. "To tell you the truth," said Kate, looking back on her early relationship with Michael, "I wasn't particularly interested in how much money he made. I was looking for someone who was not an addict, who could be faithful, and who treated me nicely."

It's All About Him

Michael treated Kate nicely at first, but as she eventually discovered, he treated himself even better. Like all narcissists, as long as things went his way, Michael could be very nice and easy to get along with. However, that was not always the case when it came to being denied something—anything—that he wanted. For example, as long as Kate didn't try to interfere in any way with Michael's activities, such as spending lots of time riding his motorcycle with friends, life was good. But if she suggested that maybe he was spending a bit too much time with his friends and not enough with her, he would immediately become testy. After he moved in with her, if she asked him to buy groceries, he'd say that business was slow lately and he didn't have the money. But Kate noted that he always seemed to have enough money to go out with his friends.

Michael also did not seem to like Kate's daughter, and tension between those two eventually became a wedge between Kate and Michael. If he wanted to do something together and Kate suggested they invite Marcella, Michael would change his mind about the activity, and then sulk. Shortly after moving in with Kate, he declared that an extra bedroom that had served as Marcella's playroom was now his "den" and promptly moved Marcella's toys into her room.

Over time, as it became clear to Kate that what Michael really wanted was to have Marcella out of the picture, her feelings for him began to cool. She tried talking to him about it, but the conversation didn't go well. It left Kate with the distinct impression that Michael had no appreciation of her love for Marcella. "I got this feeling it was all about him, that he just couldn't relate to what it means to love a child."

Indeed, for narcissists it *is* all about them. They are solidly in touch with their own feelings, but they can't empathize very well with what others feel.

Kate asked Michael to move out a little over a year after he'd moved in. By that point, she regarded him as an immature, selfish child. Besides feeling pessimistic about the prospect of meeting a man she could be happy with, she was angry with herself about having wasted a precious year because she had bought a bill of goods instead of taking more time to get a better sense of who Michael was. At the same time, she took some comfort in the thought that she had acted to save the most precious relationship she had, the one with Marcella.

The Gifted Narcissist

At those times in life when the going gets tough (and it inevitably does), the narcissist typically either quits or changes course. Usually, this response leads to a life of underachievement, as was true for Michael. However, it sometimes happens that a boy who is raised to be a narcissist is also very bright and talented. Such a boy may be able to get good grades in school despite not working very hard. He may even get recognition for his talents, again without having to persevere or overcome obstacles along the way. He is what I call a gifted narcissist.

Case Study

Sheila and Matt: The Easy Life

One example of a gifted narcissist was Matt. Good-looking and bright, he nevertheless had never applied himself with any real diligence to anything. Instead, he lived the life of a dilettante, dabbling in this and that while mastering nothing. To women, however, he presented himself as a Renaissance man of many talents. It was surprising how many women fell for that presentation. No doubt, his handsome looks and glib manner helped. He developed successful social skills, as many narcissists do, in childhood. He was the only child of parents who were well off and who did not deny themselves much either. However, whereas Matt's father had worked hard for the considerable money he earned (and spent), Matt himself was never asked to actually earn anything.

Living with a Sense of Entitlement
From an early age, Matt had tested high for native intelligence, and his potential was obvious to his teachers. Between that, his good looks, and

his interpersonal skills, he quickly grew accustomed to being their favorite. It seems that some even relaxed their expectations for him, so that he had to work somewhat less, as compared to his peers, to get good grades.

In relationships, Matt's narcissism was reflected in part in an attitude that he shouldn't have to do anything he didn't want to do, and that a "good" relationship shouldn't need much work. When Sheila met Matt, she actually thought this was an appealing, romantic notion, something akin to the phrase, "Love means never having to say you're sorry," from the film *Love Story*.

Unfortunately, as Shelia eventually discovered, for Matt this notion that a good relationship shouldn't require a lot a work only meant that he believed *he* should never have to try hard, go out of his way, sacrifice anything he wanted, or apologize for anything. That's because deep down, he believed that he deserved to have anything he wanted, and that he could do no wrong. If someone else's feelings got hurt by something he did or said, that meant they just didn't understand him.

Matt was someone who knew how he felt and what he wanted. He had refined tastes, particularly when it came to food, wine, music, and clothing. He was a known entity in several fine restaurants, where the staff would seat him at his favorite table. He seemed to be very in touch with his feelings and what he wanted to do at any given moment. All in all, Sheila took these traits as signs of an intelligent, sophisticated, and sensitive man. For a long time, she didn't see his behavior as narcissism.

Matt actually made a good living as the owner of an art gallery that catered to a wealthy clientele. His job consisted mainly of chatting up the customers, who came in already primed to buy. He told them about the various artists whose work was on display. If a piece was sufficiently

Look for True Sensitivity

Don't mistake being in touch with one's own feelings for true sensitivity. Have you ever been in a relationship with a man who was very good at articulating his own feelings and desires, but who didn't seem to be able to relate to what others felt or desired, unless what they wanted happened to be the same thing he wanted? That man was a narcissist. Some women mistake this for sensitivity, but true sensitivity is a two-way, not a one-way, street. Truly sensitive men are in touch with their own feelings, but they also can empathize with what you are feeling.

expensive, he might even arrange for a meeting with the artist. This last strategy, despite being the transparent flattery that it was, almost invariably led to a sale. Matt had purchased the gallery using money his parents had given him, and he netted 50 percent of the prices the artists received for their work—enough for him to live comfortably.

Undone by Self-Centeredness

As she got to know Matt better, Sheila began to experience aspects of his personality that took some of the shine off his persona. Although they were still dating and had made no commitment to each other, it struck Sheila as odd that Matt would make major plans—for example, to take a two-week trip to the West Coast to visit some galleries there—without even talking to her about it. He also made major purchases, such as an expensive home theater system, again without even mentioning it. She just walked into his condominium one evening and there it was. She tried to justify this by telling herself that Matt and she were just dating. Still, the lack of sharing bothered her.

Another trait that made Sheila uncomfortable was the way Matt often talked about other people. It soon became clear that he did not think very highly of many of the customers who purchased works from his gallery. He would say things like, "I can't believe they paid that much for that painting. I wouldn't have paid half as much. But better in my pocket than theirs." Or, "I wouldn't have hung that painting in my garage, much less my living room!"

Always Look at the Big Picture

Can you relate to Kate's position? Have you ever been at a place in your life when you were mostly concerned with one or two qualities in a man and tended to overlook the big picture? This is the most common way that people—men and women—get into trouble. Coming out of a bad relationship, they focus too much on the one or two qualities that made them unhappy in their last relationship and look for someone who does not have those qualities without regard to the whole person. For example, a woman who was in a relationship with a man who was stingy might be tempted to jump into a relationship with a man who is generous, only to discover later that his "generosity" is actually part of a larger tendency to be financially irresponsible and impulsive.

It seemed to Sheila that, despite his ability to charm people, Matt believed that only he knew the true worth of art, and that privately he had little respect for many of the artists whose work he touted and sold, or for the people who purchased them. Even that, though, was not enough to make Sheila reconsider the relationship. She just wrote off his superior attitude to the fact that he was obviously very intelligent.

What finally caused Sheila to take a step back and rethink her relationship with Matt was her discovery that he had accepted an invitation to a high-brow New Year's Eve party but did not invite her. When she asked him, about two weeks before, what he wanted to do on New Year's Eve, he offhandedly replied that he had already made a commitment. He then suggested, with not so much as a hint of regret in his voice, that they get together on New Year's Day. At that point, Sheila lost the patience she had come to rely on so heavily in her relationship with Matt. She asked him what this commitment was that he'd made, and why he hadn't even told her about it—not to mention talk to her about why he hadn't invited her.

"These aren't your kind of people, Sheila," Matt replied. That response got Sheila really steamed. She dug her heels in and pursued the confrontation. Looking back on it, she remembered how Matt looked truly taken aback as she confronted him. "I knew right then and there," she said, "that the biggest mistake I'd made was not confronting Matt sooner about his self-centeredness. He was actually surprised that I would dare to question his decision to leave me alone on New Year's Eve so that he could go off and rub elbows with the elite!"

Why Narcissists Can Be Attractive

Spoiled boys become narcissistic men who believe that everything they do is (or ought to be) strictly voluntary. Their interests and commitment always come first, and if you're a woman in a relationship with such a man, you quickly realize that whatever you want always comes second. You will do whatever it is that he does not like to do. In a conflict, you will always be wrong. There is little, if any, room for compromise or apology in his view of life. Finally, narcissistic men take very good care of themselves and may look marvelous, but when it comes to others, they lack generosity and often even the ability to empathize.

Despite these obvious negatives, narcissists can be appealing because they can come across not as self-centered but as self-confident. And self-confidence is a quality that many women find especially attractive in a man.

It's amazing how many women mistake narcissism for self-esteem. Unfortunately, the effects of being spoiled can be much more difficult to overcome than the effects of neglect or abuse, especially if the latter were not severe. The narcissist needs to experience a truly humbling experience if he stands a chance of reigning in his inflated ego. As the woman in his life, you probably do not want to be the person who has to provide him with such a humbling experience.

Measuring Narcissism: The Narcissism Inventory

This chapter is about identifying a second potential mistake of huge importance—making a commitment to a relationship with a man who is a narcissist. Just as abuse and neglect can vary greatly in intensity and therefore lead to varying degrees of insecurity, so can coddling vary from mild to severe and lead to a greater or lesser inflated sense of importance—in other words, narcissism.

Matt and Michael can both be described as very narcissistic men. Others are less so. That's why it is important for you to have a way to estimate just how narcissistic a man might be. Armed with that insight, you will be in a better position to decide if this is a relationship that is likely to be satisfying to you in the long run. To that end, try the following Narcissism Inventory.

Instructions

Each of the following statements describes a personality trait. Rate the man you are interested in on each of these traits, from 0 (not at all) to 10 (totally). When you are finished, total up your ratings to come up with a Narcissism Index.

1. Expects to get pretty much anything he wants.   0 1 2 3 4 5 6 7 8 9 10
2. Makes important decisions without talking to you.   0 1 2 3 4 5 6 7 8 9 10
3. Makes expensive purchases without discussing
   them first.   0 1 2 3 4 5 6 7 8 9 10
4. Acts as if he believes he is superior to others.   0 1 2 3 4 5 6 7 8 9 10
5. Refuses to apologize or make amends.   0 1 2 3 4 5 6 7 8 9 10
6. Requires frequent and extensive admiration.   0 1 2 3 4 5 6 7 8 9 10
7. Puts others down.   0 1 2 3 4 5 6 7 8 9 10
8. Lacks the ability to empathize with others.   0 1 2 3 4 5 6 7 8 9 10
9. Is preoccupied with fantasies of his own
   success, power, brilliance, or beauty.   0 1 2 3 4 5 6 7 8 9 10
10. Believes that he is "special" and can only be
    understood by or associate with others who are
    equally special.   0 1 2 3 4 5 6 7 8 9 10

Narcissism Index: ____

As with insecurity, few men can be described as not narcissistic at all or as totally narcissistic. If your honest assessment is that you are in a relationship with a man who has a Narcissism Index of 50 or higher, you need to take notice and perhaps take action.

Is He Self-Confident or Just Self-Centered?

Watch out when you are dealing with a narcissist. Beneath the veneer of what seems at first to be self-confidence is a man who thinks he's always right and should get whatever he wants. He expects life to cater to him. If he's been blessed with talent or intelligence (or inherited money), it may appear on the surface that he is almost too good to be true. The mistake you can make here is to fail to recognize that what appears too good to be true usually is too good to be true.

What Do I Do Now?

If, after reading this chapter and applying the Narcissism Inventory to a man you are interested in, it appears that narcissism is not going to be an issue, great! You can now eliminate that anxiety and move on. However, if it looks as if there is a significant element of narcissism in this man, then I recommend you move on to Part Three and apply the four critical tests to him. This will further clarify how much narcissism may prove to be a problem if you choose to pursue this relationship. On the one hand, should he pass all four critical tests, it is possible that the Narcissism Index you came up with is inflated for some reason. On the other hand, if he fails two or more tests, you probably should think twice about whether this relationship will be worth investing your time and energy.

The third possibility is that narcissism is indeed an issue you need to be aware of, but that it does not appear to be severe. In that case, the material in Part Four will be useful to you if you decide to move ahead. The most important thing to keep in mind is that you need to recognize narcissism for what it is and not confuse it, for example, with self-esteem or self-confidence. Don't fall into a pattern of relating that will make it worse.

Chapter Eight

Problem Man #3
The Beach Boy

The dominant theme in the beach boy's life (and personality) is, "Let's party!" Beach boys can be the most appealing of the problem personality types described here, simply because, for them, "Life's a beach." After all, who doesn't like to have fun?

When a woman meets a beach boy, he will most likely be around other people, having a good time. He is likely to have great social skills—the kind of person who can carry on a conversation with just about anyone. If you need help with something—anything—the beach boy is likely to know someone who can help you. He has an extensive social network.

If you're a woman who, at the moment, is not looking for a relationship so much as a man to have fun with on occasion, you may actually want to hook up with a beach boy. But make sure you have your eyes open and know what you're getting into. This is a man to have fun or a fling with, not a man to look to for a commitment.

Beach boys are fun, but they make poor mates because they are fundamentally immature and not up to the full range of adult responsibilities. They also tend to make poor fathers, because they are essentially big kids themselves. They may be good at holding down a job, but it's most likely a low-stress job that doesn't pay particularly well. Often, beach boys are impulsive spenders who don't manage money well and will spend money on friends and good times, even at the expense of other financial obligations. If they do happen to work hard, even for short stretches, they then feel that this entitles them to spend their extra earnings right away or to party that much more in their time off.

Case Study

Iris and Jacob: Dating a Playboy

Iris had just come off a disappointing break-up with a narcissist. She had known Jacob casually for some time. She considered him a friend of sorts because their social circles overlapped, but he was not someone she would ordinarily consider dating, because of his reputation for being a playboy. Iris' best friend was also friends with Jacob and liked to joke that he went through relationships "seasonally."

"Jacob has told me," the friend explained, "that he actually tells a woman that he's looking for a 'summer love' or a 'holiday companion.' When the season changes, so does his relationship! Can you believe that?!"

Also according to this friend, she knew of women who, despite Jacob's reputation, went ahead and got involved with him, only to have their hearts broken when the inevitable breakup came. They'd cry, sometimes even plead, but Jacob would be resolute. "I told you I was looking for a summer love," he'd explain. "As I recall, you agreed. I don't want to get too serious, so I think it's time to stop."

Some people might think of Jacob as a callous and calculating man; but as you'll learn in this chapter, he was really less harmful than that. He was, simply, a beach boy. Moreover, he was honest about it. He was *never* ready to get "too serious." The trap that many women apparently fell into was convincing themselves that Jacob was capable of a sustained relationship, and that their relationship would be different—with her, Jacob would change his mind about only wanting a short-term fling.

To her credit, Iris did not fall into that trap, and so she was able to enjoy a pleasant springtime romance with Jacob without allowing herself to fall in love with him. She was also not all that surprised when he arrived at her place one evening, took a seat across from her on her wide couch, and looked her in the eye. In an instant she saw what was coming and found that she was not wounded when he began talking about how "all things come an end."

Iris decided on the spur of the moment to beat Jacob to the punch. "I've been thinking about that myself," she said, "and to be honest, it's been a lot of fun, but I think it's time for me to move on. My real goal is a long-term relationship, and I know you're not the right man for that." Jacob did not appear hurt so much as a bit surprised at hearing her say that. He said he hoped they could remain friends, which Iris knew was code for being able to have sex on occasion. She gently brushed Jacob off with a vague, "Yes, maybe we will." She had no intention, of course, of taking him up on his offer.

Iris was fortunate, because she knew Jacob both personally and by reputation, and because she was clear in her own mind about what she wanted at that time in her life. She didn't try to convince herself that she could make Jacob into someone he wasn't. Her expectations for their relationship were limited, and she did not allow herself to be seduced by the fact that Jacob was a lot of fun to be with.

In contrast to Iris are all the women who fall in love with (and even marry) men who are always the life of the party, who have a wide circle of friends they like to spend time with, and who never have any trouble thinking up fun things to do. Often, these men also don't show much interest in one-on-one time together, unless that time is spent in bed.

Beach Boys and Boys' Toys

It is sometimes said the only difference between a man and a boy is the price of the toys. There may be some truth in that, and it is particularly true for the beach boy. As we get older, the cost of having fun increases steadily. Beach boys can be appealing, simply by virtue of the fact that they know how to have fun. If you happen to feel you either don't know how to have fun or haven't had as much fun as you'd like, a beach boy can be almost irresistible. Any woman is wise to find out how much time and money a man devotes to his "toys" and whether his expenditures seem reasonable, given the kind of job and income he has.

The Beach Boy Personality

Like narcissists, beach boys tend to have been somewhat spoiled as children. Many of them are an only child or the youngest child. However, though they may have been coddled, it was not to the extent that they believe that the universe revolves around them or that they can do no wrong—as narcissists believe.

Two well-worn phrases help in describing the way a beach boy is raised:

- *The apple of mom's eye.* The beach boy is typically either a mother's only or youngest child, or at the very least her favored child.
- *Don't worry, be happy.* The parents of beach boys usually went out of their way to ensure that their son had fun. His ability to enjoy life and not feel burdened by responsibilities is of paramount importance to these parents. They may not say that this is what they believe, but their actions clearly reflect it. If you look around, you can probably see this attitude in some parents you know—those who feel, for example, that school should be "failure-proof" and curricula tailored to ensure only success. They go out of their way to see to it that their son enjoys every opportunity to have fun, and that few demands are made on him.

Given this kind of upbringing, it is little wonder that the beach boy grows accustomed to having fun and not having to cope very often with frustration or disappointment. He believes that having fun is an inherited right, not something a person should have to work for. One could say that he is spoiled and has some narcissistic qualities. However, he may not think he is superior to others or spend a lot of time putting others down in order to make himself feel superior, as the narcissist does. On the contrary, the beach boy is a social animal who is everyone's friend.

The following is a nutshell description of the beach boy personality.

His Guiding Philosophy: Life's a Beach

He loves to party. Starting at an early age, responsibilities are less important than enjoying life for a beach boy. The expression, "Surf's up!" neatly sums up his approach to life: When the surf is up, it's time for him to put work aside, grab his surfboard, and hit the beach.

He Has Highly Developed Social Skills

Beach boys usually were extraverts from the time they were young. They liked the company of others more than they liked being alone. As the saying goes, they have "a way with words" and the ability to be quite charming, even entertaining.

He Wants Attention

Another implied motto of the beach boy is, "Look at me!" His social skills provide the tools for getting attention. The bottom line is that the beach boy likes to look good and likes getting attention from looking good. He is not above fishing for compliments if they don't come spontaneously.

Bad News Is Not Welcome

Beach boys love to hear good news; conversely, they hate bad news. For them, life is all about feeling good—there's no room for feeling bad. By the same token, the beach boy enjoys spending money and takes great pleasure in his toys, but he may leave the credit card bills sitting on the table and ignore the phone calls warning him that his payments are delinquent.

He Doesn't Like to Work Too Hard

For the beach boy, fun is the priority. He doesn't like to work too hard. Typically, this keeps him from achieving whatever potential he may have. The beach boy will usually either keep one relatively nondemanding job for a long time or switch jobs once the current one becomes too demanding.

Barbara and Chris: The Farm Girl and the Beach Boy

Barbara and her two siblings were raised on a family dairy farm. She described her childhood as a mixture of hard work and intense family closeness. "We were all up at 4 am, seven days a week," she explained. "I thought nothing of coming into the house smeared with mud and dung," she explained, "shedding my clothes in the mud room and hitting the shower. After that it was breakfast, and then off to school."

Despite the hard work, Barbara had nothing but good things to say about life on a farm. "We had wonderful traditions," she said, "and I think the need to work hard and as a team prepared me well for life. I feel like I'm a very self-reliant and responsible person."

As we talked about her life, it turned out that Barbara was not only self-reliant and responsible, but also a bit naive. She met Chris during her sophomore year in college. She barely dated during her freshman year. She initially found college life to be somewhat intimidating. She did not consider herself a prude, but the hard partying that took place on weekends put her off, and she ended up driving back home on many weekends. She did well, though, and decided at the start of her second year that she needed to come out of her shell.

Chris was good-looking, social, and funny. He was not exceptionally studious, but he passed his courses. They met at a party—the natural habitat of the beach boy. Barbara described it as a case of opposites attracting. Chris seemed to have the social skills and the wide circle of friends that she wished she had. She could tell that he was well liked by his male friends. He often was the one to organize social events, like driving to away football and basketball games or setting up a New Year's Eve party.

There were many times when Barbara was not included in Chris' activities because they involved only his male friends. Barbara wrote this off to the fact that they were all men, just having fun, and that none of the men took their girlfriends along on these outings.

Barbara and Chris dated steadily for three years, and after they graduated they moved in together. Rather than getting their own apartment, Chris convinced Barbara to move into his parents' home, arguing that this would enable them to save money toward a wedding and a house.

As it turned out, the savings came almost solely from Barbara's earnings. Chris spent pretty much every dollar he earned. He continued to spend a lot of time with friends and was always up for a trip to a baseball game or a sports bar. Again, Barbara found herself bothered by this at times, but if she brought it up, Chris' reply was that he and his friends were just having innocent fun, and maybe Barbara should think about doing the same with some of her friends. The problem was that, compared to Chris, Barbara had a small circle of friends, more and more of whom were getting married and exiting the singles scene.

Wife and Mother

When, after a year and a half of living with his parents, Chris brought up the idea of marriage, Barbara said yes. Looking back on it, she believed she did this partly because it was what all her friends were doing, and partly because she thought that marriage might help Chris to settle down. She was, of course, wrong. Nevertheless, she went ahead with the marriage, and within a few months she was pregnant. Though she would not have described herself as especially happy with her marriage, Barbara found motherhood very rewarding, and by their fourth anniversary, she and Chris had two daughters who took up much of Barbara's time. A trained paralegal, Barbara continued to work, but only part-time from home to help out with the finances, while Chris became the primary breadwinner.

Chris earned a good salary as a salesman of office equipment. His salary came mostly from commissions he earned on volume sales to corporations and state agencies. Despite his earning capacity, however, once Barbara stopped working full-time, their savings account stalled. Chris continued spending money freely on social activities, in particular, season passes to baseball, basketball, and football games. He would purchase not one ticket, but two. What with two toddlers to care for, babysitters in short supply, and a tight budget, Barbara was not in a position to go to many of these events. Besides, it had always been obvious to Barbara that Chris preferred to do these things with his male friends; sometimes he would invite a customer he was courting. That was how he justified spending a couple of thousand dollars a year on sporting events. "It's a great way of sealing the deal with a prospective customer," Chris would argue. Barbara conceded that this might be true, but what about all those times when Chris just went with friends? He countered by claiming that "most of the time," the friends would reimburse him for the price of the ticket (which he would then promptly spend on drinks and food).

Meanwhile, having lived in Chris' parents' home for six years, Barbara was beginning to feel decidedly claustrophobic. Their space consisted of two bedrooms and a bathroom. They had to share the kitchen, laundry, and family room. Needless to say, this arrangement afforded the couple very little privacy. Even their bedroom abutted that of Chris' parents.

When she finally reached the limits of her patience and confronted Chris with how intolerable this situation was becoming for her, his response was the usual: He promised to spend less and save more so that they could afford a down payment on a house. But Barbara had heard this promise many times before, and after six years, they still were short of what they needed.

As usual, it was evident that Chris wasn't about to change his behavior to match his words. In fact, as she discovered when she was cleaning out the pockets of one of his coats before putting it in the wash, Chris had developed a new hobby: casino gambling. Again when confronted, he countered, saying that he visited the casino only rarely, and only to meet friends for a quick meal and an hour or so at the most at the blackjack tables. He'd do this, he said, at times when he knew in advance that his sales calls happened to land him close to a casino. Moreover, he argued, over the past year he had "pretty much broken even," although exactly what he meant by "pretty much," he didn't specify.

Although Chris had his paychecks deposited into a joint account from which Barbara paid the bills, she knew that he also earned money under the table. She had no idea how much this was, but she believed it was considerable, since Chris tapped into his paycheck in order to purchase tickets only about half the time. If she asked him about his under-the-table income, though, he would get irritated. "I need to have some of my own money!" he'd snap at her. "I work hard enough for it! I deserve it!" This reaction smacked of a beach boy throwing a tantrum when someone tries to take his surf board away or tells him it's time to stop surfing and go to work.

Leaving the Beach Boy Behind

When Barbara was finally frustrated and unhappy enough to bare her soul to her parents, they insisted on "loaning" the couple enough money to bring their savings to the point where they could afford a down payment on a modest but comfortable house in a pleasant community. Now, three years later, Barbara was feeling as frustrated and unhappy as she was back then. The problem, from her perspective, was that she and Chris still had no "marriage" to speak of. "He has a life," she explained. "He has fun with his friends just like he did before we were married. In fact, life for Chris hasn't really changed all that much in eight years. But I have no real life, other than for the girls, and Chris and I certainly have no life together as a couple." In other words, Chris continued to live the life of a beach boy, leaving Barbara to be the responsible adult in the family. It was a role she was well groomed for, but it wasn't her idea of a marriage. She didn't particularly like the resentment that was building up inside her. "I realized I was starting to feel sorry for myself," she explained, "and I don't like that quality in people."

Chris was minimally involved in taking care of the children. For example, he had never taken either girl to their pediatrician, and didn't even know the doctor's name. He did not have car seats in his vehicle, using the excuse that he needed the back seat for sales materials. He never cooked or cleaned. He did not even mow the lawn—that, too, was Barbara's job!

Chris was not an abusive father, but neither was he an attentive one. As Barbara had discovered was true for their marriage, when it came to his relationships with his daughters, Chris would always put his own needs and interests first. If one or the other wanted to come along when he had something to do, that was fine. But he would never go out of his way to do something they wanted to do. So they ended up doing very little with their father.

Chris' stock excuse for being selfish—that he "deserved" his toys and had "earned" his distractions—had long since fallen on deaf ears with Barbara. She felt lonely and unhappy for a long time, and eventually became alienated from Chris and resentful of his selfishness. She finally told Chris that she was seriously thinking about a divorce and went so far as to consult an attorney. She had been thinking about it for a couple of years, but wanted to wait until the girls were both in school full time so that she could go back to work.

How Much of a Priority is Partying?

Because she was relatively naive, and because she had been raised to be a responsible worker, Barbara did not initially see Chris's interest in spending so much time having fun with friends as a warning sign of things to come. Many women make this mistake, believing that having reservations about how much time a man spends with his friends amounts to being a wet blanket. On the one hand, it is fine for men (and women) to have friends that they spend time with. In fact, having a network of same-sex friends can be vital in times of crisis. On the other hand, try to be aware of what the agenda is for this social network. If it extends beyond merely having fun—for example, being supportive—fine, but if partying appears to be the only agenda and a man devotes lots of time to it, don't expect that to change if and when you get more involved with him.

Shocked, Chris responded with what struck Barbara as genuine surprise that his wife was so unhappy. He offered to go for marital counseling, but Barbara's feelings for him by then were so damaged that she told him she was not interested in doing that. She preferred, she said, to just go their separate ways.

Dont Wait Until All the Love Has Been Squeezed Out of You

If Barbara made a mistake, it was in not speaking up sooner. By the time she finally confronted Chris with her profound unhappiness, it was already too late to salvage their marriage. Not that he would necessarily have changed if Barbara had confronted him a year or two earlier, but at least Chris would have had the opportunity to make a choice. As it was, Barbara was put in the position of appearing to spring her unhappiness on Chris, giving him no chance to change. That allowed him to play the victim, which he did—which, in turn, only made Barbara feel guilty. Had she not waited so long and instead let Chris know earlier that she was falling out of love with him, she would not have had to carry this burden of guilt.

Case Study

Anne and Dave: A Lack of Serious Intent

Anne had been a good student and a responsible young woman for as long as she could remember. At the same time, she saw herself as someone who didn't know how to have fun and who always hesitated when others went out and enjoyed themselves. For example, as an undergraduate, she attended a college that was only a short drive from the beach. On warm, sunny Fridays, many of her classmates would hightail it out to the beach as soon as they could, even if it meant missing Friday afternoon classes. But Anne held back. Rather than hopping in a friend's car and heading for the warm sand, she would head for the library and put in a couple of hours of work. Only then would she drive herself to the beach.

It was not hard to understand why, in her second year of law school, Anne was attracted to Dave. They met—appropriately enough!—

at the beach. He was a year older and quite handsome ("dashing" was the old-fashioned but accurate word that came to Anne's mind) and fun-loving.

The son of well-off parents, Dave worked in the family business and had also briefly attended law school before taking what he described as a "leave of absence." Anne was quite taken with Dave, who thought nothing of spontaneously taking a day off in the middle of the week to hit the ski slopes and who liked to plan exotic vacations. She quickly allowed herself to indulge in fantasies of how much fun life would be with a man like Dave. Over the next six months, she felt that they became very close and were probably on their way to a long-term relationship.

On a whim one day, Anne decided to check out the Internet dating sites to see if Dave had a listing on any of them. When the first two she tried came up empty, she actually felt relieved. She realized then that what she was really doing was trying to reassure herself that Dave was serious about their relationship.

You can imagine Anne's surprise, then, when she looked up Dave's name on a third dating site and his picture and biographical sketch popped up. Dave described himself as follows:

Hi. I'm Dave. I am a native of the West Coast. My favorite activities include skiing, hiking, biking, and wind-surfing. I'm living on the East Coast now because I'm attending law school. I am financially independent. I am someone who believes that as important as success is, there is more to life than hard work. I'm interested in meeting an intelligent woman who shares some of my interests and my philosophy and who is interested in dating and/or a potential long-term relationship.

If He Seems Too Good to Be True, He's Probably Too Good to Be True

This is a corollary to the idea that "what you see is what you get!" In describing himself on the dating site, Dave was simply taking advantage of what millions of others have taken advantage of—the ability to create a persona that advertised him to the world. He was, in a word, *fishing* for women. And as transparent as his ad was, no doubt there were women who were willing to take a bite at the bait. Don't be such a woman!

Needless to say, Anne was devastated. It was like someone had pulled the rug out from under her. But she also had the good sense to call a couple of friends, who came over right away. She cried as she told her tale. Then one of her friends asked to read Dave's description. When she did, she broke out in laughter. Then the other friend read it and also laughed. "Mr. Too-Good-To-Be-True!" the friend said. Then Anne laughed, too. "That's just what I was telling myself not two weeks ago!"

Taking Stock of a Beach Boy: The Beach Boy Inventory

This chapter includes examples of men who could be described as fairly extreme beach boys to help you understand what this problem personality is all about. Some men are the kind of beach boy that Chris was, but others are less severe cases of this personality type. What you need to do is decide how much of a beach boy a particular man might be. You may decide that you are willing to tolerate a little of this kind of personality, but not a lot. You may also have discovered after reading this chapter that you have wasted precious time pursuing a relationship with one or more beach boys, only to feel resentful and alienated, as Barbara did, in the end.

Instructions

Use the following inventory to create a Beach Boy Index for a man you are interested in. Score each descriptive statement from 0 (does not apply to him at all) to 10 (fits him to a tee). When you're done, add up the individual scores to come up with your Beach Boy Index.

1. Enjoys taking risks.	0 1 2 3 4 5 6 7 8 9 10
2. Doesn't like to work too hard.	0 1 2 3 4 5 6 7 8 9 10
3. Is financially irresponsible.	0 1 2 3 4 5 6 7 8 9 10
4. Having fun is his first priority.	0 1 2 3 4 5 6 7 8 9 10
5. Does not like to be tied down.	0 1 2 3 4 5 6 7 8 9 10
6. Makes spur-of-the-moment decisions.	0 1 2 3 4 5 6 7 8 9 10
7. Avoids confrontations.	0 1 2 3 4 5 6 7 8 9 10
8. Likes to party.	0 1 2 3 4 5 6 7 8 9 10
9. Justifies extravagance as "deserved rewards."	0 1 2 3 4 5 6 7 8 9 10
10. Is always looking for a new toy.	0 1 2 3 4 5 6 7 8 9 10

Beach Boy Index: ____

As most people read through this list of personality traits, they agree that at least some of them can be attractive. Finding risk exciting, for example, is partly what activities like surfing and hang-gliding are all about.

Being spontaneous can be appealing to the woman who tends to hang back. These same qualities, though, are also what drive millions of people to spend billions of dollars in casinos every year. However, it's all a matter of degree. The man who never takes risks, who fears spontaneity, and who has a narrow circle of friends is surely not very appealing. Many people would call him a stick-in-the-mud. Women whose self-image tends to go in this direction may be especially drawn to men whose personality seems to offer an escape from the doldrums.

What Do I Do Now?

So, just how much of a beach boy can a man be and still be worth your time and effort? As a guideline, I'd consider any Beach Boy Index higher than 50 a clear red flag. If that's the case, you should ask yourself the following questions:

- Am I attracted to this man because he seems to know how to enjoy life and I think I don't?
- Am I trying to convince myself that once he commits himself to a relationship with me, this beach boy will put away his surfboard and settle down?

As before, I'd urge you to go on to Part Three and apply the four critical tests for a relationship to this man you are interested in. If he passes them all with flying colors, you may want to consider moving forward. However, if he fares poorly on these tests, you'd be wise to keep on looking. Remember, being selective is a better long-term strategy than simply trying to market yourself. The less time you waste pursuing poor candidates for a long-term relationship, the more chance you have to meet Mr. Right.

Chapter Nine

Problem Man #4
The Addict

There is little doubt that we live in a time that could be called "the age of addiction." Perhaps at no other point in history has a society been as much the victim of addiction as ours is today. From gambling to drugs to the Internet to text messaging, exercise, dieting, and interactive games, Americans from ages eight to eighty are increasingly getting hooked on something in an addictive way.

Ironically, many of our contemporary attitudes support, or *enable,* addictions of all kinds. It is, for example, considered not just acceptable but almost admirable these days to be *driven.* Most people put in longer workdays than their parents or grandparents did. Not just a few actually take pride in this, and some go so far as to boast about answering work-related emails at 1 am! Many people today approach other activities, such as exercise or dieting, in this same driven way.

The cardinal quality of addition—any addiction—is that it progressively consumes more and more of a person's life, thereby leaving less and less room for other activities and commitments. As the addict forms first a *friendship* and then a *relationship* with the object of his addiction and gradually progresses to a *commitment* to it, other relationships find themselves squeezed out. Addiction throws our lives out of balance and inevitably leads to negative consequences that make life unmanageable.

Common Characteristics of Addiction

Most people are accustomed to associating the word *addiction* with alcohol or drugs. However, examples of other kinds of addiction, all of which satisfy the previous definition, are easy to find. Just visit a casino and observe how many gamblers are glued to the card tables and slot machines. Visit a health club and see how many people don't just exercise, but spend almost as much time building their bodies and gazing at their reflections in the mirror as Arnold Schwarzenegger did in the film *Pumping Iron.*

Survey your friends and colleagues to identify those who work 60 hours or more a week, or who are all but obsessed with what they eat and how much they weigh. You may know someone who appears to be addicted to his handheld Internet device or who spends countless hours playing Internet games, checking out the blogs, or visiting sites like MySpace and YouTube.

There are so many kinds of addiction that one might be tempted to conclude that there are no common denominators connecting them. But addicts share several common characteristics. Obsession is one, here are some others.

Denial

It is common knowledge among professionals who work with addicts that addiction is not only a progressive disease, but one that is characterized by denial. In other words, the addict is blind to his own addiction, as well as to how it gradually but increasingly takes over his life. From the addict's point of view, nothing at all about his life is unbalanced, much less out of control. He views his addiction as a hobby, an interest, or an obligation. "I have to work as much as I do," he may say, or, "I just enjoy working out for three hours every day." The more the addict defends himself or accuses others of trying to interfere with his life or control him, the worse his addiction is likely to really be.

Addiction is insidious. No one wakes up one morning and says to himself, "I think I'll become an addict today." No one sets addiction or loss of control over one's life as a goal. Rather, addiction is something that creeps up on a person. However, because it is progressive and not an all-or-none kind of thing, it is possible to estimate just how far along the road to addiction a man has gone.

The Addiction Inventory included at the end of this chapter yields an Addiction Index that you can use to estimate how much of an issue addiction of one kind or another might be, or become, in a potential relationship. Of course, the higher the score, the farther along the addiction is and the less likely that a man will be able to pull out of it unless he recognizes it for what it is and makes a determined effort to create more balance in his life.

Ironically, the woman who is in a relationship with an emerging addict may find herself accused of trying to control that man or of interfering with his lifestyle. In truth, such defensiveness may actually thinly mask an existing or emerging addiction that will progressively consume both the man and your relationship. It is the addiction, in other words, that is "controlling" the man, not the woman in his life.

Sadly, some women have fallen victim to addiction in a desperate effort to save such a relationship. They may begin drinking or turn to tranquilizers in order to reduce their stress or anger. Some may even join the addict in an attempt to have more time together.

Look for a Balanced Lifestyle

A friend once said to me, "No one leads a balanced lifestyle these days!" Although that may be true, surely there are degrees of imbalance. Once you've spent even a little time with a man, it shouldn't be difficult to get a gut feeling for just how balanced or unbalanced his life is. To do this, look for how much time he devotes to each of the following: work, recreation, family, friendships, and hobbies. Imagine an old-fashioned pie graph, and divide this man's various activities into slices of the pie. No doubt some slices will be larger than others, but beware of slices that seem to make up almost all of the pie!

A Compulsive Streak

When adult addicts look back on their lives, they are usually able to recognize addictive tendencies that were part of their personalities even as children. Some may recall being compulsive about certain rituals in their lives. These are the people who may have gotten caught up in avoiding cracks in the sidewalk, who needed to say a certain number of prayers before they could go to sleep, or who needed to follow a rigid routine every morning. Others can remember being compulsive about how they arranged their toys or dolls in their bedroom. The word *compulsiveness* succinctly captures this core aspect of the addictive personality.

Not everyone is compulsive. Moreover, being compulsive is not a totally pathological quality. On the contrary, it probably isn't possible to become, for example, a really good nurse, physician, engineer, or architect without having some compulsiveness as part of your makeup. In fact, our culture values compulsiveness, as long as it is limited to being organized and efficient. You certainly wouldn't want to undergo surgery performed by someone who is not organized and efficient! You probably also would not want to find yourself on the top floor of a skyscraper designed and built by people who were not at least somewhat compulsive.

But compulsiveness can get out of hand and become the tail that wags the dog.

Jack: Man on a Treadmill

Jack was 36 and divorced. A pharmacist, he had a job that he enjoyed and that paid him fairly well. Like many others in his profession, he had to be organized and somewhat compulsive. After all, to a degree, people's lives were literally in his hands. Many of his customers were on multiple medications, and he needed to be especially vigilant for potential drug interactions that could be dangerous. In Jack's job, mistakes could be costly.

You could consider Jack's vigilance in his work to be a positive kind of compulsiveness. Still, as useful as it was for him and his clientele, it nevertheless was a core aspect of the addictive personality, and in his case, it set the stage for dysfunctional addictions. Ironically, these were addictions that, like his vigilance at work, initially seemed not only harmless but healthy. They had to do with diet and exercise.

Jack took up jogging at the suggestion of a woman friend, a fellow pharmacist. He was looking for something to fill the time he had on his hands since his divorce and for a way to change his lifestyle. He began slowly, jogging at a relaxed pace for half an hour three mornings a week before going to work. At the same time, he consulted a nutritionist to get some advice about how best to shed 15 pounds and stay healthy.

All went well for about a year. Jack lost the weight and then some, and after a year he was running almost every morning for nearly an hour. He decided to have his body mass tested to check the ratio of muscle to fat. At that point, he somehow slipped over the line that separated healthy diet and exercise from addiction. Looking back, he saw how a contributing factor was the breakup of another relationship that began about six months earlier. He had high hopes for that relationship, until the woman told him that it was missing something for her and that she decided to accept a transfer to another part of the country to be closer to family.

Within another year, Jack's running turned from exercise to compulsion, and his interest in health and diet became an unhealthy obsession with what he could and could not eat. He stopped going to restaurants completely and started preparing his own meals, and became very picky about what kinds of food he bought and where he bought it. He read up on diet supplements and, before long, was swallowing 10 to 12 pills each day. He then decided that, in addition to running, he needed to get involved in a regular exercise program to strengthen his muscles. He joined a health club, consulted with a personal trainer, and embarked on a conscientious and demanding program of exercise that included weight lifting.

By this point, Jack's life was mostly taken up with work, running, exercise, and his concern with his diet. That was pretty much the whole pie, and it left little, if any, room for friends, much less another relationship. His attitude toward running and physical fitness went from being interested in getting in shape (a relationship) to feeling that he needed to run 365 days a year, regardless of how bad the weather might be, or even if he might be ill (a commitment). It meant having as little body fat as humanly possible. No matter the conditions—outside his house or inside his body—Jack would roll out of bed at 5 am each morning, don his jogging gear, and hit the road. He rarely skipped his exercise program.

Jack's preoccupation with fat was so severe that several of his friends (with whom he spent less and less time) expressed alarm about how thin he was. In an effort to help him break out of the trap he'd created, they invited him for dinner. On several occasions, they also used these invitations as an opportunity to invite a single woman to introduce Jack to.

To their frustration, Jack's friends found that he'd show up for dinner as invited but eat next to nothing and then leave early. His usual excuse was that he needed to get to sleep so that he could get up at 5 am to run. The women he met would report that even if they went so far as to call Jack after meeting him and suggest getting together for a walk or a cup of coffee, he would either not return their call or be noncommittal about getting together.

Jack is a good example of how easy it can be for what starts out as a healthy interest or activity to turn into an addiction. The process is usually not precipitous, but insidious. Again, no one "decides" to become an addict.

The Role of Anxiety and Depression

In order for addiction to take root, two things need to be present. The first, already mentioned, is that the individual has a compulsive streak in his personality. Jack surely exhibited that.

The second thing needed for addiction to emerge is *anxiety* or *depression*. Inevitably, addictions arise as a way of avoiding one of these two painful emotional states. In Jack's case, it was depression that pushed him toward addiction. It began after his divorce, which had not been his idea, and it had taken a decided turn for the worse after the subsequent relationship he had such hope for turned sour.

The proof that addiction is often a way of avoiding anxiety or depression is what happens when an individual attempts to recover from an addiction. Inevitably, when he tries to give up the addiction, the addict is flooded with anxiety, depression, or both.

Holly and Taye: Living with a Gentle Workaholic

A prominent consequence of addiction is a steady stream of losses. As addiction takes over an individual's life, it gradually takes up a bigger and bigger piece of the pie. Eventually, it can take over the whole pie, squeezing out everything else. Work suffers, relationships suffer, and in the case of some addictions, health suffers as addiction takes over the individual, much the way a hostile vine or insect can gradually squeeze the life out of a tree.

Compensating for a Childhood of Neglect

Taye wasn't exactly raised with a silver spoon in his mouth. When he was four, his father literally took off in the middle of the night, never to be heard from again. The few things he could recall about his parents' marriage were mostly memories of angry, raised voices, and some pushing and shoving. When he was eight, his mother decided to surrender her parental rights, and Taye and his older brother were placed in what amounted to a state-run orphanage. He never learned the exact reasons for this, though for a long time he suspected that his mother was an alcoholic and had gotten into trouble for neglect.

According to Taye, the orphanage was not really such a bad place to live. At least the meals were regular, and he had clean sheets and a warm bedroom. That was more than he could say for what his mother provided. On the other hand, an orphanage is not a home, and paid caretakers are not family.

Taye told how he initially walked around feeling as if there was a heavy rock permanently embedded in the pit of his stomach. That feeling no doubt represented the loss of his attachment—such as it was—to his mother. He and his brother saw her rarely, and briefly, on holidays and their birthdays.

Compulsiveness made its appearance early in Taye's personality. He remembered clearly how he had a reputation for keeping the neatest room in the house and for always being sure his clothes were clean and pressed (even his jeans). He was a very conscientious student who got straight As and was active in every team sport that the institution offered. In his spare time, he tutored other boys who were struggling with their schoolwork. He got lots of recognition for these activities, and, understandably, they came to form the basis of his identity and self-esteem. He was, in a word, a worker.

Whereas many of the other boys he grew up with went on to live lives of frustration and disappointment, Taye was a model of success. He went to college on a scholarship, then to graduate school (also on a scholarship) to study physical therapy. He met Holly when he was doing an internship in a rehabilitation center where she worked as a receptionist. Neither one had very much dating experience, but they hit it off well, and a year later married. Two years later, they were the proud parents of a beautiful daughter.

Things went along fairly smoothly for the next couple of years. Holly's only concern was how much her husband worked. She'd been aware since she'd met him that work played a big role in Taye's life. She knew about his past as well and understood the role that work and helping others played in helping him succeed against all odds. She found him to be a gentle man who had modest expectations and was easy to please, but who avoided conflict and even the slightest confrontation. But she appreciated the fact that Taye's willingness to work overtime whenever it was available was what allowed her to stay at home with their daughter while enabling them to buy a condominium.

Over time, Holly couldn't help but notice that Taye spent increasing amounts of time working, leaving her and their daughter alone more and more. And the older the girl got, the more Taye worked. He would be gone before she got up in the morning and would return home long after she was asleep. If overtime was available on the weekend, two full weeks might go by before Taye's daughter laid eyes on her father.

Resisting the Control of Anxiety and Depression

What Holly did not realize was that Taye was being driven into addiction not only by the compulsive streak that was part of his personality, but also by the anxiety and depression that would set in whenever he would spend time at home. No doubt, these emotions were stirred up because he never had a family life himself and had no idea how to make one. In contrast, Holly came from a large family that had remained close despite the inevitable moves that modern life demands. They got together for holidays and arranged reunions. She knew that Taye was uncomfortable in these situations and could sympathize. But she still insisted on going. And though Taye went along and tried his best to socialize, the truth was that he couldn't wait for these family gatherings to end so he could return to work. He once confessed to Holly that if he could, he would gladly work two shifts a day, seven days a week.

Things came to a head for Holly when their daughter was six. Christmas was coming, and Holly told the girl it was time to write her wish list to Santa. The girl went to her room and came back five minutes later with only one item on her list: "I want my father to stay home more."

The note jolted Holly. She understood her own loneliness. The word *workaholic* came up in conversations between her and Taye more than once. She knew that he had gotten caught up in a web of some sort that he either could not or would not get out of. At the same time, work was not alcohol, drugs, or gambling. Her friends sympathized with her plight, but a couple of them also remarked on occasion that they wished their own husbands were as "ambitious" as Taye. So Holly had come to terms with the fact that being married to Taye meant not having much time with him.

When she realized how much Taye's absence was hurting their daughter, however, Holly could hold her tongue no more. She confronted Taye with the Santa note. He read it and she saw tears well in his eyes. "We need to get help," she told Taye. "You grew up without a family. I won't let that happen to our daughter."

Confronting Taye's Addiction Head-On

Overcoming his addiction was hard work for Taye. It was a struggle for him to set any limits on how much he would work. Adding to his difficulty was the fact that the agency he worked for was chronically understaffed, so that overtime hours were virtually always available, both during the week and on weekends. Try as he might, Taye could not seem to keep himself from signing up for overtime. He'd promise Holly, and then break his promise every time. Eventually, this led to some heated arguments and accusations. Holly would accuse Taye of loving work more than he loved her or their daughter. Taye would angrily respond that Holly did not appreciate the benefits that his hard work brought the family.

Taye did not really make any headway in overcoming his addiction until Holly asked him to move out. On the one hand, she realized that others might think she was crazy, asking a man to leave not because he was

Love Alone Won't Heal an Addiction

Holly made a mistake that many partners of addicts make, which is to hold back and hope that their relationship—in other words, love—will be enough to save the addict from his addiction. Actually, the opposite is more likely: The addiction kills the relationship. The best way to begin dealing with addiction is to acknowledge it for what it is and to recognize how powerful it is. As the example of Taye's workaholism shows, the individual's willpower alone is usually no match for the compulsion that drives an addiction.

a cheat or an alcoholic or an abuser, but because he was a workaholic! On the other hand, she also knew what the consequences of Taye's addiction had been for her and their daughter. She knew it was a risky gamble, but she felt in her gut that Taye needed to be on his own in order to get some perspective on what he had given up.

Taye did move out, and the shock of that was enough to motivate him to get counseling from an addictions specialist. He also became involved in a fellowship of people who were struggling to overcome addictions of their own. It was not easy, but after a year, Taye finally had a foothold in recovery. He understood that his addiction was driven by the profound depression that had been caused by his abandonment, and that he covered it up through becoming such a hard worker. He also understood how the compulsive part of his personality had paved the way to addiction. Fortunately for him, once he got a taste of what it was like to have a relationship with a loving child and confronted the painful emotions that this relationship released within him, he was able to make gradual progress toward creating a more balanced lifestyle.

Addiction Is a Story of Loss

Although Holly did not express it in exactly those terms, on some level she instinctively knew that Taye needed to get a sense of what he was losing because of his addiction. Efforts to protect an addict from experiencing such losses are called *enabling.* By asking Taye to leave so that he could get some perspective on what he'd pretty much already lost to his workaholism, Holly was actually doing him a favor.

The Subtle Slide From Friendship Into Slavery

Interestingly enough, addiction begins as something that is functional. Only over time does it take over a person's life and destroy it.

To illustrate how addiction starts out as a good thing that eventually turns bad, consider the most common addiction—alcoholism. People start drinking for one of two reasons: Either it makes them feel good, or it helps them escape from a negative emotion, typically anxiety or depression. The shy person may find that a couple of drinks make it easier for him to tolerate social situations that he would otherwise avoid. The uptight person may find that a couple of drinks allow him to relax and laugh. And so on.

At that stage of use, alcohol could rightly be called a *friend*. As with any friend, you enjoy the company and look forward to spending time together. At this friendship stage, however, what could eventually become an addiction is not in control of your life. Like any friendship, it is only part of your life. Typically, those who are close to the future alcoholic do not have much of a reaction to his "friendship." In fact, they may even think it's a good thing.

As the individual gradually develops a tolerance for alcohol, he needs to drink more in order to get the same effect. Similarly, the workaholic gradually needs to work even more and make even more money in order to feel good, and the gambler begins to make bigger bets in order to get the "gambler's high" that comes with winning. This is the point at which a person begins to head down the slippery slope to addiction. This is also usually the point at which the individual is becoming dependent on alcohol (or work, or dieting, or gambling) to either feel good or to avoid feeling bad. You could say that he now has a *relationship* with alcohol (or whatever the eventual addiction will be).

This relationship then begins to compete with the man's other priorities for his time and attention. Understandably, those who have been his priorities until now, and who were previously tolerant of his drinking, begin to experience jealousy. However, they often hesitate to express it. They may try to justify the drinking (just as the drinker does) by saying to themselves something like, "Jack just likes to have a drink or two," or in the case of gambling, "Jack has a good time at the casino." By rationalizing the drinking (or gambling), they are trying to console themselves.

If unchallenged, the addiction will, in time, progress from a relationship to a *commitment* that takes precedence over the man's former interests and other responsibilities. In the commitment stage of addiction, the drinker does not like to be far from a drink, and the gambler likes nothing better than to find excuses to visit the casino. He may even say he likes to hang out there because he likes the food. In reality, he and the object of his addiction have now become inseparable. The alcoholic, for example, will keep his supply well stocked and will become anxious if he begins to run low. He will not want to go places where drinking is not allowed. He may even begin to keep a secret supply. Finally, he will become moody and irritable if he has to go without a drink for even a single day.

For obvious reasons, significant others begin to move beyond jealousy and experience downright resentment as the drinker enters the commitment stage. They are resentful because they are being pushed out of the alcoholic's life. He spends as much or more time either drinking or thinking about drinking than he spends with them. And when he is with them, his consciousness is affected by the alcohol. In Taye's case, it was painfully apparent to Holly that when her husband was at home, he was uncomfortable and was thinking about work.

Sadly, it is often not until addiction has progressed to the commitment stage that the addict fully realizes what is happening to him, even though it probably has been obvious to those close to him for a long time. By then, however, his relationships with friends, family, and co-workers may be so alienated that they can't be repaired. And if it is alcohol or drugs that is the object of addiction, there may be significant physical consequences as well.

Perhaps you have had the experience of getting into a relationship with an addict. Maybe you have a friend who seems to be caught up in such a relationship. Today more and more men seem to be addicted to the Internet. They gradually lose control of their ability to set limits on how much time they spend at the computer. They sacrifice sleep, neglect family responsibilities, and even lose interest in sex. The object of their Internet addiction may be pornography, but it can also be online gaming or shopping, or Internet sites where he (and women) create false personas and develop "relationships." There are men who literally fall in love with an imaginary Internet lover.

If this sounds familiar, then you understand how much of a man's time and energy addiction sucks up. To avoid wasting valuable time and energy, you owe it to yourself to be aware of addiction and how it progresses, and to honestly assess how far along a man might be in the addiction process. If his addiction is at the friendship stage, that's one thing. You shouldn't ignore it, but you may still have a chance to build a relationship with this man. However, if he seems to have a commitment to his addiction, don't fool yourself into thinking he will easily give up that commitment for you.

Measuring Addiction: The Addiction Inventory

Keeping in mind that addiction is something that evolves gradually and does not emerge full-blown overnight, it is possible to assess how far addiction has progressed in a man. Keep in mind also that addiction applies not just to alcohol or drugs but can be centered around many different things. The examples used in this chapter—severe cases of exercise, dieting, and work—are also addictions.

Instructions
You can use the following Addiction Inventory to estimate where a man may be in the addiction process. Rate each statement as it describes him, from from 0 (not at all) to 10 (totally). The activity referred to can be

drinking, taking drugs, exercise, gambling, the Internet—just about anything that appears to play an increasingly major role in this man's life. Add up the scores to come up with an Addiction Index.

1. Relies on this activity to feel good. 0 1 2 3 4 5 6 7 8 9 10
2. Seems to rely on this activity to avoid feelings such as anxiety or depression. 0 1 2 3 4 5 6 7 8 9 10
3. Becomes a major priority in his life. 0 1 2 3 4 5 6 7 8 9 10
4. Makes him irritable or upset if he has to give up this activity for even one day. 0 1 2 3 4 5 6 7 8 9 10
5. Arranges his life so as to be able to engage in this activity. 0 1 2 3 4 5 6 7 8 9 10
6. Places higher priority on the activity than on relationships. 0 1 2 3 4 5 6 7 8 9 10
7. Is unable to set limits on how much he engages in this activity. 0 1 2 3 4 5 6 7 8 9 10
8. Neglects responsibilities in order to engage in this activity. 0 1 2 3 4 5 6 7 8 9 10
9. Allows this activity to throw his life out of balance. 0 1 2 3 4 5 6 7 8 9 10
10. Seems "married" to this activity. 0 1 2 3 4 5 6 7 8 9 10

Addiction Index: ____

Remember, It Isn't Only Alcohol

This point has already been made, but it is vital to keep in mind that alcohol and drugs are only one kind of addiction. The discussion in this chapter can just as easily be applied to work, dieting, exercise, gambling, and sex, to name a few common addictions. The important thing to remember is that addiction progresses: from relationship to commitment to slavery.

What Do I Do Now?

If you answered all of these questions honestly (not minimizing any of them), you should now be able to assess whether addiction is (or may become) an issue in this relationship. An Addiction Index of 50 or higher is a reason to be concerned. This man may already be on the path to addiction. Very low scores generally mean that addiction is not an issue, and you can relax. Middle scores, say between 25 and 45, suggest that you'd be wise to keep an eye on this activity to see if it progresses over time toward addiction. It may be just a "friend" right now, but don't let yourself become complacent about the role of this particular friend in this man's life.

If the Addiction Index is 50 or higher, you should now turn to the four critical tests for relationships presented in Part Three and apply them to this man. In addition, a litmus test to determine whether addiction may be a threat to a potential relationship is the degree to which the man's life seems to you to be *balanced*. One way to evaluate this is to create a pie graph that represents this man's life. Divide the pie into "slices" that represent each of the following areas of living:

- Work
- Play
- Exercise
- Relationship with a significant other
- Family
- Friends
- "Addictive activity" (drinking, drug use, gambling, etc.)
- Hobbies

Your pie graph will give you a quick visual image of where you and your relationship fit into this man's lifestyle. Remember that although I've included a category called "addictive activity," some of the other areas on this list also have the potential to evolve into addictions, including exercise and play.

We all face competing priorities in our lives. But for our overall mental health, as well as for the sake of having a fulfilling relationship, each of these areas must have its place in the pie. Addiction is something that progressively takes over more and more of the pie. It starves relationships of the time and attention needed to sustain them.

Chapter Ten

Problem Man #5
The Control Freak

When she first began dating Max, Nikki was impressed not only by the fact that he was a successful medical professional but that he seemed so organized. He owned a home that was spotless ("You could eat off the floor!" she'd boasted to her friends) and maintained a regular routine of caring for it, both inside and out.

Case Study

Nikki and Max: A Relationship Lost to Rigidity

When Nikki and Max first met, he was engaged in a major project, building a half-acre pond in a sunny corner of his four-acre plot of land. He was doing some of the tasks himself while contracting out the heavy work, such as bulldozing. Nikki was touched by Max's story of how as a youth, he and his family had lived for several years in a house by a pond, and how sad it was when the family had to relocate to another part of the country and he was forced to leave the pond behind.

Nikki's previous relationship had been with a man who was as disorganized and lacking in ambition as Max was organized and goal-directed. She'd even gotten the impression that this fellow might be looking for someone to support him in his endeavors. So the contrast was both striking and intriguing. She was a professional herself—a computer programmer—whose work, like Max's, demanded organization and attention to detail.

It wasn't until they'd been dating steadily for 10 months or so that Nikki began to notice—and feel uncomfortable about—some of Max's ways and habits. The first thing that struck her was how slowly his pond project was progressing. The problem seemed to stem from the fact that Max was so caught up in every minor detail—he wanted the pond to be absolutely perfect—that he had trouble settling on a decision and moving along. He'd postponed some of the work so many times that one contractor already quit, saying he had many other commitments and he couldn't wait on Max any longer.

Another thing that started to bother Nikki was Max's habit of cleaning up after her, without giving her a chance to do it herself. For example, if she stayed over and he made breakfast, he would clean his dishes and put them away even while she was lingering over her breakfast. And no sooner would she eat the last bit of toast than he would scoop up her plate and clean it as well. Such scenarios made Nikki think of the comedy *The Odd Couple,* and at first she tried to get over her annoyance by telling herself that she was better off being with a "Felix" than an "Oscar," referring to the fictional neat and sloppy roommates.

Yet another thing that Nikki found annoying about Max was his stinginess. Initially, the fact that he suggested splitting expenses like restaurant bills and the price of concert tickets did not really bother Nikki. At least, she thought, Max was willing to pay his share. And sometimes he would pick up the tab, especially if it wasn't too expensive. As with his other habits, Nikki tried to put a positive spin on Max's miserly nature, telling herself it was better to be frugal than to be a spendthrift.

The thing that finally began to concern Nikki the most about Max, though, had nothing to do with his apparent perfectionism, his miserliness, or even his excessive tidiness. Rather, it was the rigidity of his thinking, specifically his beliefs and values. From Nikki's perspective, it was one thing to be moral and scrupulous. She felt that she had decent values herself and tried to live by them. But Max's ideas about right versus wrong struck her as overly rigid, almost cruelly so. She believed, for example, in the concept of mitigating circumstances, and in compassion and mercy. But when Max would talk about people he would be incredibly judgmental, and it was obvious to Nikki that his morality left no room for mercy, compassion, or the idea that under certain circumstances, a violation of rules might be judged leniently. Not so for Max, for whom the moral world was strictly divided into black and white, good and bad. He would talk about people he knew, people he worked with or who worked for him, and people who were mentioned in the news. Nikki found that she had to bite her tongue many times, for if she ventured even a mildly different opinion, Max would pounce on her. At such times he would be downright condescending, as if Nikki obviously did not know right from wrong.

As time went on, Max's rigidity and need to control everything began to wear on Nikki. She tried to get his pond project moving along by making a suggestion or two and then encouraging him to make a decision, but he would listen and then do nothing. Eventually, as the pond remained little more than stakes in the ground and a blueprint that had been redone a hundred times, Nikki began to suspect it would be a long time—if ever—before she would see water, lily pads, and frogs in Max's backyard. She stopped expressing her opinions about others' behavior after he dismissed her opinion for what seemed like the hundredth time. And she found that she stopped thinking about how she might redecorate Max's house if they were to be together, realizing that he would never allow her to make a single change without his approval, which she sensed he would not easily grant.

As you might have guessed would happen, Nikki ended her relationship with Max after concluding that she could never be happy living with a man whose world was so controlled and rigid. Fortunately, she had not yet invested too much—only a little more than a year of her valuable time. She counted herself lucky that her personal counselor had pointed out some of the traits about Max that bothered Nikki, named them for what they were, and asked Nikki to consider how unlikely it was that they would change as a result of Max being in a relationship with Nikki. When the unavoidable conclusion was that she would not be able to change Max's personality, Nikki opted to go her own way.

Organized or Controlling?

Do any of Max's traits sound familiar to you? Does he sound like a man you've been in a relationship with in the past or are interested in now? Equally important, can you identify with what Nikki did, which was to make excuses or try to put a positive spin on Max's personality? In fact, such words as *intolerant* and *controlling* described Max's behavior better than words like *upstanding* and *organized*. The distinctions drawn by the use of such terms are more than mere words—they are significant differences that can make or break a relationship.

The Control Freak: A Personality Sketch

Naturally, Max did not think he was a control freak. Rather, he saw himself as an organized, responsible man who kept his life in order, had good values, and was financially responsible. This is more or less the story that all control freaks try to sell to the world. Many women buy into it. And if you are not involved with a control freak, that is how they can appear, at least when viewed from a distance. However, the view from inside a relationship with a control freak is quite different. From this inside perspective, such a man has the following traits.

Hung Up on Details

This man can get so caught up in details, lists, or schedules that it is difficult for him to get anything done. If he is interested in planning a vacation, for example, he may become so preoccupied with where it should be, what the itinerary should be, how he should get there, and what to take along that it takes him forever to finally make the trip happen. His preoccupation with details, planning, and organization can take all the joy out of the vacation. One man who needed a new roof for his house obsessed for so long about what kind of materials to use that the old one leaked severely in a hurricane causing a couple thousand dollars worth of damage to the walls and ceilings.

Perfectionist

The control freak is such a demanding perfectionist that he may have a hard time completing things. Projects around the house can stand unfinished for months or even years as he waits to get them done perfectly. He may even undo what he's done and start over from scratch if the project doesn't meet his standards. As a corollary to this, he is highly critical of others and is quick to point out their faults and imperfections.

Moody

The control freak is plagued by moodiness that is a direct result of his perfectionism and excessive need to control things down to the smallest details. Life, of course, will not comply with this man's desire for perfection and control, and as a result he is chronically frustrated, stressed, and moody. Some people describe control freaks as prone to brooding.

No Room for Spontaneity

This person is committed to plans and routines. His week is usually mapped out ahead of time, and once established, his routines rarely change. He does the same things, in the same order, time after time. Only if something new or different is planned well in advance will he be able to accommodate that change without feeling uncomfortable. He is so committed to routine and to sticking with a plan once it is made that he can get very upset, even explosive, if forced to change it.

Intolerant and Morally Rigid

Being conscientious may be a virtue, but this man carries it to an extreme that can be stifling. He sees the world in black-and-white, good-versus-bad terms. In judging others' actions or beliefs, he embraces rigid rules that leave no room for consideration of mitigating factors. He is very uncompromising and is more interested in "fairness"—in other words, in holding everyone to the same rigid moral standard, regardless of extenuating circumstances—than he is in "justice." He shows little compassion for human foibles or for those who err or make poor choices.

A Hoarder

He holds on to worn-out or worthless possessions, even if they have no sentimental value. He may argue that something that clearly ought to be thrown out may come in handy later. He resists cleaning out his house in this way, and while his personal space may be extremely organized and neat, he also tends to accumulate things that just take up space.

Stingy

The control freak is a miserly sort who is reluctant to spend money on others. He does not experience the joy that motivates others to give. Making a child smile by offering a gift is not something he goes out of his way to do. He regards money as something to be stockpiled for a potential future emergency and is preoccupied with the idea that others may try to "rip him off" in one way or another.

Cannot Delegate

This trait is especially evident in the workplace, though it can also rear its ugly head at home. Since he is a perfectionist, the control freak has a hard time delegating tasks to others or working as part of a team, because in his heart he believes that only he can do it right.

Stubborn

The word stubborn nicely captures the essence of the control freak. By stubbornness, I mean the trait of being unwilling to compromise, insisting on having his own way, and not being open to influence from other people. The more stubborn a man appears to be, the more of a control freak he is likely to be.

As a woman enters a relationship with a control freak, she will find herself increasingly feeling as if she were in a psychological prison. Unfortunately, this process is often a gradual one. The control freak sees himself in a much more positive light, and a woman may initially buy into that self-image. That is what happened to Jessica.

Jessica and Andrew: The Strangling Grip of Control

Jessica thought of herself as a woman who got burned in relationships because she'd always been attracted to the type of man I call a beach boy. Jessica regarded herself as a fun-loving individual who had nothing against partying. However, at age 30 she came to realize that men who thought life was one continuous party might be fun to be with for a while, but they were not candidates for a long-term relationship. So she set about looking for a man who was "mature" and "serious" about life. She let her friends know that this was what she was looking for. She signed up for an Internet dating service, filled out her psychological profile indicating her preferences, and waited for the matches to start rolling in.

Jessica was an attractive, petite woman who was also talented and the successful co-owner of a popular salon and day spa. Doing well in that business requires not only a good head for business, but also good social skills and a certain flair, all of which Jessica possessed in abundance. She'd gone to college to study business and gotten her degree, but after several years of trying to work her way up a corporate ladder, the opportunity to co-own the salon presented itself and she went for it.

Jessica was introduced to Andrew by one of the salon's customers, who had written her first book and was celebrating with a book party. Andrew was a professor of English at the same college where the newly minted author also taught. Jessica's first impression of Andrew was that he was good-looking, though a bit on the slender side compared to the men she was typically attracted to. He was also soft-spoken and obviously intelligent. He owned his own home, a modest but attractive colonial in a desirable community, and he enjoyed biking and sailing a small, two-person sailboat on local lakes. Jessica suspected that as a professor, Andrew made less money than she did through the salon; on the plus side, he was tenured and had job security.

Andrew would later tell Jessica that he was attracted to her because of her liveliness and disarming smile, her good sense of humor, and her striking good looks. She also seemed to him to be mature for her age. Andrew had what he considered to be several disappointing relationships and was looking to settle down with someone intelligent that he could both talk with and have fun with.

At that point, Jessica had no idea that Andrew was a control freak for whom fun, like everything else in his life, had to be carefully planned and followed to a T. So when he told her that his last vacation was to visit the rainforests in Costa Rica, she thought that sounded like great fun. She did not know the excessive lengths that he had gone through to plan that trip, the detailed and rigid itinerary he'd stuck to, or the fact that he nearly had a breakdown when a violent rain storm caused him to change his plans and make an unplanned overnight stay.

Jessica found her early dates with Andrew to be enjoyable. She noted that he was not exactly the spontaneous type but would talk with her several times beforehand about where they might go and what they might do. But this didn't really bother her very much. In a way, that was better, she told herself, than being with someone who just made things up as he went along. When she visited his house, she noticed that it was filled with neat piles of journals, books, and magazines, many of which were old and which she would have thrown away without a second thought. When she offhandedly asked Andrew about them, he replied that they were magazines he subscribed to and hadn't finished reading. Did he think he would some day get around to reading them all? Jessica asked with a laugh, since it seemed to her an unlikely if not impossible task. She was taken aback when Andrew snapped back that it was up to him to decide.

Seeing the Problem with Control

After the incident with the magazines, Jessica found herself hesitating to speak her mind quite so spontaneously around Andrew. Instead, she would hesitate and think about how he might react if she said what was on her mind.

As she got to know Andrew better, Jessica discovered that while from an outside perspective it might seem that he had it all together, in reality, his personal life and even his professional life didn't fit that image. Her friend told Jessica that Andrew was widely regarded by his colleagues as a teacher who was exceptionally bright, if somewhat demanding. Although the drop-out rate from his courses—known for their rigor and organization—was higher than average, those students who finished his courses spoke highly of him. From Andrew's perspective, any students who were too lazy to do the work he expected of them or who were looking for "an easy A" were making a mistake if they registered for a course with him. Jessica thought that this made sense, though she never actually attended one of Andrew's classes.

Increasingly, Jessica saw Andrew as a man who, in his personal life, often got bogged down in details, whose perfectionism slowed him down, who was often moody, and who sometimes had trouble making what she regarded as relatively minor decisions, such as where to go or what to order for dinner. He also labored over his teaching responsibilities. He would spend so much time grading and correcting students' papers that it became an onerous task. It was so painful to Andrew that he would often put off sitting down and doing it until the last minute.

The first time that Jessica really bumped up against Andrew's controlling personality, aside from the magazine incident, was when they made plans to take a hike on a park trail. At the last minute, Jessica felt a strong urge to instead take a scenic drive through the country to a café that had outside seating. She thought it would be fun to linger, talking, over a leisurely lunch.

Andrew became visibly uncomfortable when he arrived to pick up Jessica and found that she was not dressed in her hiking clothes. When she happily told him about her idea of substituting her plan for the one they'd agreed on and to go on the hike the next day, Andrew testily replied that they should go for the hike as planned and go to the café the next day if she still wanted to. Jessica could sense that Andrew was rather angry at her for this last-minute change. She also sensed that going to the café would be no fun, given Andrew's current state of mind, so she agreed to change her clothes and take the hike. She also decided to drop the idea of going to the café for lunch the next day.

As Jessica got to know Andrew better her own, more spontaneous personality began to rub up against his highly controlling nature.

The next incident occurred one sunny Sunday, when they'd planned to take their mountain bikes for a ride through a state park that featured a number of biking trails. As usual, Andrew had carefully mapped out their course and made copies for both of them.

At one point during their ride, Andrew was ahead of Jessica and disappeared over a ridge. When Jessica got to the place where she'd last seen Andrew, the trail split in two and went off in different directions. She turned off and headed in the direction she thought Andrew had taken. A few minutes later she realized she had gone the wrong way and headed back. When she arrived at the fork again, she found Andrew sitting on the ground beside his bicycle, with a look on his face that actually frightened Jessica. "Where did you go?!" he demanded. Before she had a chance to explain what she had done, he pulled the map out of his back pocket, flashed it at her, and said, "Can't you read?!" Hearing those words and the tone in which they were spoken was enough for Jessica. She mounted her bike and, without saying a word to Andrew, headed back toward their starting point.

After the bike-riding incident, Jessica was not sure she wanted to continue dating Andrew. But her best friend and business partner suggested that Andrew was probably just scared and reacted with anger.

"It's like if I tell my son to meet me at a certain spot in the mall at a certain time and then he's not there and I have to wait for him. By the time he gets there I'm worried to death, and when I see him I'm both relieved and angry." Jessica could understand that. However, she saw an important difference: She was not Andrew's child, but a grown woman. She believed she was owed an apology. When she told him so, Andrew surprised her and did apologize, so she decided to continue the relationship. Privately, however, Jessica was now more than a little wary.

The Final Straw

Jessica and Andrew had planned (as usual!) a quiet dinner in his favorite restaurant. Jessica had gotten used to the routine of planning these things, including not just where they would go and when, but who would be paying. They often split the expenses, but this time Andrew said it would be on him.

They were in the middle of their entrée when Andrew began talking in what struck Jessica as a rather demeaning way about some of his students. He complained that so many of his students had never read any books of note, could not write a coherent sentence, much less a paper, and were in effect pretty much a waste of his valuable time. "But isn't that what they're going to college to learn?" she asked. "I mean, are they expected to come to college with those skills already in hand, or is it your job to teach them those skills? It's sort of like the women who come into the salon. Many of them have no idea of how to make themselves look attractive. That's why they come to the salon, to have someone teach them that."

According to Jessica, Andrew rolled his eyes and replied, in a very condescending tone, "With all due respect, Jessica, that's the kind of analogy that one of my students might make."

That comment ended the conversation for Jessica. She said she experienced an urge to get up and walk out, but forced herself to finish the meal. No sooner had Andrew paid the check, though, than she said she had a headache and felt ill. She asked Andrew to just drop her off at home instead of going back to his place. She sensed he knew that something was wrong, but he didn't pursue it.

Jessica thought long and hard about her relationship with Andrew and the various interactions that troubled her. In the end she decided that, despite the fact that most of her friends thought he was a "keeper," she did not want to continue the relationship. She had already begun to feel constricted when she was with him, and she strongly sensed that it would probably get worse, not better, the longer they were together.

Measuring the Need to Control: The Control Freak Inventory

As is true for all of the personalities described in this book, there are degrees of the need to control. There is even a range of needing to be in control that could be considered healthy. Think about it. What would your life be like if you absolutely gave up all need to have some control over it? You'd be like one of those silver balls in a pinball machine, bouncing around wherever the bumpers and flippers happen to send you. You may know some women whose lives seem to operate that way, and no doubt you do not envy them. That said, let's look at the point at which the need to be in control goes from something that is functional to something that can kill a relationship. To begin, read the following instructions and then complete the Control Freak Inventory.

Instructions

Use the following inventory to create a Control Freak Index for the man you are interested in. Score each descriptive statement from 0 (does not apply to him at all) to 10 (fits him to a tee). When you're done, add up the individual scores to come up with your Control Freak Index.

1. Can get so hung up in details that things don't
always get done or get done late.   0 1 2 3 4 5 6 7 8 9 10
2. Perfectionist; can get bogged down by wanting
things he does to be perfect.   0 1 2 3 4 5 6 7 8 9 10
3. Critical; points out faults and imperfections
in others.   0 1 2 3 4 5 6 7 8 9 10
4. Moody; prone to mood swings, including
depression and anger.   0 1 2 3 4 5 6 7 8 9 19
5. Morally rigid; sees the world in black-and-white
terms and judges others by rigid standards of
behavior.   0 1 2 3 4 5 6 7 8 9 10
6. Married to routines and plans; has a hard
time changing plans or routines.   0 1 2 3 4 5 6 7 8 9 10
7. Hoards; keeps things long after they have
outworn their usefulness.   0 1 2 3 4 5 6 7 8 9 10
8. Cannot delegate; resists delegating to others
because they will not live up to his standards.   0 1 2 3 4 5 6 7 8 9 10
9. Miserly; is not generous with gifts or money.   0 1 2 3 4 5 6 7 8 9 10
10. Stubborn; is uncompromising and unyielding. 0 1 2 3 4 5 6 7 8 9 10

Control Freak Index: ____

Biting Your Tongue Can Be Bad for You

The first sign of trouble ahead was when Jessica found herself feeling hesitant to say what was on her mind when she was with Andrew. Having disagreements or opposing opinions does not kill a relationship; rather, it is feeling that it is not okay to disagree or have an opposing opinion. The control freak acts as if his opinion is the only opinion that matters, or the only way to do something. If you feel inhibited about saying what you think or believe (assuming that you're not doing so to be mean intentionally), then you need to take that very seriously. Sooner or later, the habit of biting your tongue is going to lead you to feel alienated and resentful.

What Do I Do Now?

Since at least some need to be in control is normal, scores on this scale of 40 or less may not be cause for concern. This may just be a man who understands that he needs to have his life somewhat organized, that he needs to plan and not be a spendthrift, and that doing things well usually leads to rewards and recognition.

Now let's consider scores in the middle range, say between 40 and 60. Look at the items on which the man's scores are highest. What does this say about him? Do any of these represent areas where you feel uncomfortable in this relationship? Have you attempted to address them at all, and if so, how did that conversation go? Is he open or not open to looking at himself? Generally speaking, scores in this range are an indication that you would be wise to apply the critical tests for relationships, described in Part Three. These critical tests, combined with the index you come up with, may help you decide if you want to pursue this relationship further. If you do, then Part Four gives you some tips on what to do (and not do) in a relationship with this kind of man.

Finally, a score on this inventory of 60 or higher typically spells trouble. If you've been in the relationship long enough, you may already know this. If it's a relatively new relationship, you'd be smart to consider what lies ahead. Unless you happen to be a woman who sees her role in a relationship to be that of a follower, you may end up feeling like a prisoner. See how this man does with the four critical tests. And keep in mind that a man with a really high Control Freak Index is not likely to change.

Chapter Eleven

Problem Man #6
The Predator

You could say that I've chosen to save the worst for last in presenting this sixth and final type of problem man. Some people actually don't believe there is such a thing as a predatory man—as if human beings are somehow the exception to the rule that exists in the rest of the natural world. There are, however, predators throughout nature, and they've existed throughout time. They exist today, and not only in what we like to call the "animal kingdom."

As is true elsewhere in nature, human predators seek out the vulnerable and often stalk their victims. You may believe that you have been the victim of a predator one or more times in your life. In this chapter, we look at how to identify a predator, hopefully before you become his next prey. If you choose to pursue a relationship with a man who appears to have a predatory streak, Part Four looks at the issue of your vulnerabilities and what you can do to reduce your chances of being exploited.

The Predatory Personality

The predator is identifiable through a number of personality traits. These same traits may be evident to a lesser degree in people who are not truly predatory; however, they will be much more pronounced in the predator. You will be able to use the Predator Inventory, presented at the end of this chapter, to estimate just how predatory a particular man may be.

The Usual Rules Don't Apply

The predator may not say it in so many words, but through his actions he reveals his belief that the rules most people live by just don't apply to him. He may go so far as to think people who live by society's rules are naive or stupid. The rule he lives by goes something like this: "If you can get away with it, do it." He has little compunction about breaking the law if that will benefit him and if he believes he will suffer no negative consequences. Intelligent and talented predators have embezzled millions of dollars from the corporations they have led.

Deceitful

The predator lives by his own rules and does not hesitate to lie or con others for his personal gain or pleasure. For example, a predator may create several different Internet profiles in order to lure women. Depending on which one he thinks will appeal to a particular woman, he may be a physician, professional skier, or teacher. Again, talented and intelligent predators can be very convincing at presenting the face they want to present. The bottom line for him is that he gets what he wants, whether it be sex, money, or something else.

Aggressive

It goes almost without saying that the predator is aggressive. Whether he is born that way or learns that aggressiveness gets him what he wants, the predator is pushy and persistent in pursuing his goal. Most people do not like confrontations and tend to experience anxiety in the face of anger, and the predator knows from experience that aggressiveness will get him what he wants most of the time. Extremely predatory men, like their animal counterparts, seem capable of sensing anxiety in others and respond to it by becoming more aggressive.

Stalker

Predators seek out the vulnerable: women who are lonely and want companionship, who are insecure and crave praise and encouragement, who have been abused and seek comfort—even women who are vain and vulnerable to flattery. The predator is uncanny in his ability to identify and exploit a woman's vulnerability, to get whatever he wants or can get from the relationship. Once the predator identifies a vulnerable woman, he may even stalk her until he gets her—though not necessarily stalking in the sense of literally following her. Rather, the stalking often takes more subtle forms, such as striking up a friendship, showing up "coincidentally" at places she goes to, or pretending to have a common interest they might pursue together.

Unable to Empathize

Predators want what they want and don't particularly care what others may want or how others may be hurt by their exploitation. In their words or actions, they reveal an attitude that it's just their victims' "tough luck" if they feel hurt, exploited, or abused. They can do this because they do not identify with how others may feel; they only know how *they* feel. If a predator severely hurts a woman's feelings and she cries, he will not feel sad. On the contrary, he may get angry or even laugh at her tears.

Lack of Remorse

Just as the predator doesn't empathize with how you feel, he does not regret things he does that may exploit or hurt you. Rather, the predator blames the victim. If you are hurt or exploited, it's your fault for being naive or gullible. Viewed through the predator's eyes, the world is divided into two classes of people: survivors and victims, or con artists and marks. From his point of view, the Latin phrase *caveat emptor*—buyer beware—applies to all human interactions. If you get taken in, or taken advantage of, it's your own fault. Any apology the predator may make is designed to do nothing more than placate you or, worse, to set you up to be victimized again.

A Rare Phenomenon?

When I talk to groups about predators, invariably someone in the audience accuses me of exaggerating. Surely, they argue, predators as I describe them either don't exist or are very rare. My reply? Think again. As you look back on your past relationships, do you believe that you got involved with one or more predators or at least had a close call with one? Do you believe you were ever identified and stalked by a predator, including some of the more subtle forms of stalking described here? Predators are real, just as sharks, wolves, eagles, and tigers are real. To some, they may even have their place in the food chain. However, my goal in this book is to be able to identify and avoid them. In order to do so, though, you first have to believe in them.

Case Study

Jennifer and Jeff: A Blast from the Past

Jennifer was raised in a modest, blue-collar family. Her parents earned every dollar they made and appreciated what they had. The oldest of four children, Jennifer became responsible at an early age. She remembered having fun growing up, but she also recalled having to take on such responsibilities as doing the laundry, cleaning up after meals, and supervising her younger siblings' baths. Like her parents, she grew to appreciate what she had and was never extravagant.

Jennifer worked hard in school, was a better-than-average student, and after finishing high school earned an associate's degree from a local community college. She then took a clerical job in the county's only hospital, and after 10 years had worked her way up to a position as assistant office manager in the pediatric department. Never married, Jennifer had only one serious relationship in her life so far. It ended when the man decided he wanted to leave the semirural area where he and Jennifer had lived their whole lives, whereas Jennifer decided she wanted to stay. Then she met—or rather, remet—Jeff.

Jennifer and Jeff knew each other in high school. He was something of a cut-up back then, getting into more than a few scrapes with the authorities, but as far as Jennifer recalled, it was nothing more serious than that. Jennifer remembered that she had been attracted to Jeff despite (or maybe because of) his spotty reputation. He reminded her of the character played by James Dean in *Rebel Without a Cause*.

Jeff left the area after finishing high school, and Jennifer knew nothing about him after that. Then one day, out of the blue, he showed up again.

Jennifer first heard from an old friend that Jeff was back in the area. Jennifer said she was "somewhat interested" when she heard the news.Then, she found herself even more interested when her friend revealed that Jeff expressed interest upon hearing Jennifer's name.

Then one day, Jennifer came home to find a message from Jeff on her answering machine. He sounded friendly enough, describing the call as a "blast from the past" and saying that if she was up for it, he'd like to get together for a cup of coffee or lunch. That seemed innocent and safe enough to Jennifer, so she called Jeff back and accepted his invitation.

An Old Attraction Rekindled

Their initial lunch date went well. Jennifer and Jeff continued to see each other on a regular basis, and Jennifer soon found her old attraction to him rekindled. She noticed that he did not talk much about what he'd done in the years he'd been away, and that whenever she brought it up, even casually, he managed to change the subject. He did say that he had held a few jobs in "management," but was vague about the details. He also told Jennifer that he'd gone to school to study business but was equally vague when it came to details. He said that the reason he returned was that he'd gotten "homesick" and that he had an older sister who was his only family and who still lived there with her husband and three children.

What Jennifer discovered later was that Jeff had seen his share of trouble since leaving town. He did indeed take a few courses, but had never come close to getting a degree. He had lived with a succession of women, all of whom he'd taken advantage of financially, either by allowing them to support him while he was "between jobs" or by outright stealing money from them. In one case, he memorized a woman's password when she did her online banking. Just before he disappeared suddenly from that woman's life, he went online and transferred several thousand dollars to an account he had opened using a fictitious name, then went to the bank and withdrew it.

Though she could not see it at the time, Jennifer realized that Jeff must have sensed that, as "the girl left behind"—who stayed in her home-town and never married, despite her dream of having a family of her own—she was vulnerable. For his part, Jeff seemed to know the right things to say, and though she should have known better and seen through him, Jennifer chose to believe that Jeff was being sincere when he said, for example, that he also always wanted a family but life had just not cooperated.

Jeff told Jennifer that some stocks he was planning on cashing in had lost almost all of their value because a global company went bankrupt, thereby causing him a "temporary" cash flow problem that stood in the way of his getting an apartment. She suggested he move in with her for the time being. By then, they'd been dating steadily for eight months or so and were intimate. They'd even begun to talk about a future together. Again, what Jennifer didn't know was that Jeff's sister, who had been put-ting him up all that time, told him it was time for him to move out.

A Turn for the Worse

After Jeff moved in with her, Jennifer's life quickly took a turn for the worse. Though they were intimate before Jeff moved in, once he was there, Jeff acted as if it were Jennifer's duty to have sex with him every night. Then he started becoming critical of the way she looked. Jennifer already had her doubts and insecurities about her appearance (her nickname for herself was "plain vanilla"), and Jeff appeared to sense this vulnerability and played on it. Whenever they went out, for example, he would point to some other woman, compliment her on how she was dressed and made up, and say something like, "Now, you should try out a look like that."

The months went by and still Jeff did not find a job. Jennifer's friends began asking questions and expressing concern. Jennifer told them the same thing that Jeff told her: that he'd been told he was "overqualified" for the local jobs he applied for. Of course, Jennifer had no way of know-ing if this was true or not—until a friend told her that Jeff had not applied at all for a job he said he'd interviewed for. When she asked Jeff about this, he flew into a rage, telling her, "Keep your nose out of my business!" He accused her friend of being a meddler and said that all of Jennifer's friends were against him and were set on breaking up their relationship. He said that Jennifer should "kiss them off."

After living with Jeff for six months Jennifer was feeling depressed, depleted, and defeated. Her self-esteem was lower than it ever had been. She now saw herself as a loser—someone whose dream of a happy family life would never be realized. She was miserable with Jeff, yet despite the fact that she supported him financially, she felt powerless to get him to leave. Then one day, just as suddenly as he'd appeared in her life, he left. Disappeared. When she got home from work one Friday, Jeff and his things were gone, along with several hundred dollars of "emergency cash" that she thought was hidden in her bedroom closet. As relieved as she was when several hours passed and she realized that Jeff would not be walking through the door, Jennifer felt a wave of sadness wash over her. She lay down on her bed and cried quietly for about an hour. Then she called a friend, who came over right away, along with her husband and a new lockset for Jennifer's front door.

Can you identify with any aspect of Jennifer's story? Has there ever been a time in your life when you, like her, were vulnerable? What was the nature of that vulnerability? How did someone take advantage of it?

Jennifer's was a classic case of a woman who fell victim to a fairly slick predator. She was by no means a failure in life, but she did have her vulnerabilities and insecurities. Her life so far had definitely not fulfilled her dreams. It's easy to imagine how Jeff, returning to his hometown after many years, could easily have found out some basic information about Jennifer and singled her out as prey. He may even have known she'd been attracted to him in the past. At first, he flattered her with attention, and then gradually took advantage of her good nature to live off her for a while.

Other predators who are not as subtle or clever as Jeff rely instead on simple intimidation. However, they still identify their prey as being vulnerable women, then single them out, and hunt them down. One such man was Richard, who, like Jeff, also preyed on a woman he'd known before.

Case Study

Susan and Richard: Living with "The Bully"

Richard previously had a succession of brief and unsuccessful relationships. In his 50s and a carpenter by trade, he also had moved around the country quite a bit, never staying in one place longer than a couple of years. It was shortly after making yet another move, this time to return back East, ostensibly to be closer to family, that he met Susan. She had recently divorced a man—an alcoholic and a gambler—who could not hold down a job for long and who repeatedly ran them into debt. Nevertheless, Susan had stayed with him for 10 years. It was her second marriage (the first one ended after five years due to abuse), and she was left with a son and daughter to raise by herself.

To say that Susan was insecure is putting it mildly. Although her children appeared to be turning out alright despite the upheavals in their lives, and though she had a good job as a researcher in a highly successful law firm, Susan privately thought of herself as a "two-time loser."

Susan met Richard through the Internet. He described himself as a skilled carpenter (which he was) who lived in several different places (which he had) but was now looking to settle down. He had no children and was not looking to start a family but was interested in finding a compatible companion. That sounded nonthreatening enough to Susan to warrant a response. They exchanged a number of e-mails over a two-week period. Looking back on those exchanges, Susan realized that she had disclosed much more about herself, including her divorces and her struggles to raise two children while working full-time, than Richard had revealed about himself. She remembered thinking that, with respect to not talking much, maybe Richard was just being a "typical man."

When they finally did meet—for lunch in a public place, as recommended by the dating Web site—Susan thought Richard was, for his age, a very attractive man; "well preserved" was the way she put it. He was neat and clean. She noticed that his hands were somewhat rough and worn-looking, but then, he was a carpenter. He was very polite and again kept the conversation focused more on Susan than on himself. He mentioned that he was temporarily living with a niece and her family until he got himself set up with permanent full-time employment and a place of his own.

In many ways, Susan's story from this point on is very similar to Jennifer's experience, though Richard turned out to be even more aggressive than Jeff and, unlike him, didn't conveniently disappear. Within a couple of months, Richard moved in with Susan. He got a job as a carpenter but refused to share living expenses other than to give Susan a weekly check for $100 that he said was his contribution toward the food and utilities bills. Once in a while, he would help out by doing minor repairs around the house. However, he always gave Susan the bill for any materials he needed to purchase for the job. His largest contribution to the household by far was to replace an aging deck that was beyond repair, but in that instance, too, Susan had to reimburse him for the cost of the lumber, nails, and other material.

Susan's son was away at college when Richard moved in, but her daughter, Gretchen, a junior in high school, was still living at home.

Gretchen and Richard took an instant dislike to one another. She avoided him as much as possible, which was not that difficult to do—between schoolwork, friends, and the sports she played. Richard made no secret, however, of his opinion that Gretchen had it too easy and that she should get a job and contribute to the household expenses.

The True Colors of a Predator Start to Show

It wasn't long before Richard began to show his true predatory colors. He was an ornery man who knew what he wanted and would not hesitate to be aggressive in getting it. He never hit Susan but was verbally abusive, accusing her not only of spoiling her children, but also (ironically) of being "controlling." This hurt Susan, because when she first met Richard she disclosed that her second husband had made the same accusation. Of course, it was Richard who was the controlling one in this relationship, but Susan was confused. She didn't realize that Richard leveled this accusation at her only when he wanted something and she resisted.

It wasn't long before Susan's children settled on the nickname "The Bully" for Richard, though they didn't use this moniker much in front of their mother, out of consideration for her feelings. The few times she tried talking to Susan about Richard, Gretchen found her mother defensive and clearly uncomfortable.

Susan put up with Richard for more than a year. That was when he started pressuring her to quit-claim half of her interest in her house to him. He said that since they were a couple (though not married), he deserved that. In addition, he promised that if she gave him a 50-percent interest in the house, he would begin paying for half of their expenses. At around that same time, he started referring to the deck he'd built as "sweat equity." Susan listened to what Richard had to say, but each time he'd bring up the issue, she would feel a knot in the pit of her stomach and put him off by saying she would think about it.

When it got to the point that Richard was bringing up the issue of signing over half of her house to him two or three times a week, Susan finally bit the bullet and said that she'd given it a lot of thought and decided that she would not do that. He threw a fit. He cursed her. He hurled the "controlling woman" accusation at her yet again. But by then this accusation was beginning to lose its effect, and Susan simply stood her ground. The house was something she'd managed to pay for through all the years she worked to support herself and her children. It was the one thing that she and they could look at and know that it would always be there. So Richard could keep his money, she said, and she would keep her house.

Richard did not disappear from Susan's life. Instead, he started staying away more. And when he was home they spoke less and less. Then their sex life, which had been dwindling, came to a halt. When she noticed him spending more time on the computer, Susan suspected that Richard might be looking for someone else. When the day came that he walked into the kitchen and told her he was leaving, she felt sad but not really surprised. She was sad, she explained, not because she would miss Richard, but because she had wasted so much time on him and exposed her daughter and son to his nastiness.

The qualities that predators have in common are very evident in the first two vignettes. As is true in nature, predators seek out the vulnerable and try to separate them from the support of others. They stalk them, often taking advantage of whatever insecurities and self-doubts they may harbor. Finally, they devour their prey, taking advantage of whatever the relationship can do for them, while giving back as little as possible.

Trust Your Gut Instincts

It seems that just as predators have a sort of sixth sense for identifying vulnerable prey, most people have something of a sixth sense that warns them that a predator is close by. The trouble is, people don't always trust their instincts, partly because they don't believe in predators. For Susan, that sixth sense was the knot that she got in her stomach when Richard wanted her to sign over to him an interest in her house. Luckily for her, she trusted that instinct, stood her ground, and refused. You would be wise to do the same, as the following example shows.

Case Study

Zoe and the Predator: A Happy Ending

Zoe described herself as having two seemingly incompatible passions: clothes and frugality. Ever since adolescence, she had managed to satisfy both passions by shopping at consignment stores. She could quickly assess such a store to determine if its owner stocked quality items. If so, she would put the store on her list of places to visit on a more-or-less regular basis. As a result, she could boast an extensive wardrobe that didn't even come close to breaking her budget.

While shopping for herself, Zoe would sometimes look for a good shirt for her younger brother or her father. They were always appreciative of these little gifts and would marvel at Zoe's ability to purchase an attractive designer label shirt for just a few dollars. Her brother joked that people he worked with teased him for being extravagant. "I never tell them that you got the shirt I'm wearing for two bucks!" he told Zoe.

One day when Zoe was visiting one of her favorite consignment stores, she noticed a man who appeared to be, like her, 30-something, poking through the men's clothing. They made eye contact, and he smiled. Zoe returned the favor, then went about her usual business of looking through the racks of clothing.

Zoe was intently examining a work dress when she suddenly felt uneasy. Looking up, she found the man standing beside her, a bit too close to her liking. She backed away a step. The man smiled again. He had a nice smile, she thought, and didn't look threatening at all. Then he asked her if she would mind giving him her opinion as to which of two shirts he was holding would look better on him. Zoe looked at the shirts, then asked the man to hold each one up to his chest. It was clear to her that one of them looked much better than the other and she said so.

The man thanked her and then attempted to strike up a conversation. He introduced himself as Alan and said he thought it was great fun shopping in consignment stores. He dropped a hint that he actually made a lot of money and shopped in this particular store for fun, not out of need. Zoe, feeling a bit uncomfortable again, just nodded. She didn't reveal anything about herself other than her first name. She then politely excused herself, making a brief comment to the effect that she was on a tight schedule.

A minute later, Zoe was at the cash register writing out a check to pay for her dress. Suddenly Alan again appeared at her shoulder and, as before, she felt he was too close for comfort. But he merely thanked her politely for her advice about the shirt, which he bought. As Zoe left the store, she glanced back over her shoulder. Alan was looking at her and smiled. She smiled back weakly, then headed straight home.

The Calls Start

It was a few days after the incident in the consignment store that the phone calls started. It was Alan. He left several pleasant enough messages on Zoe's voice mail: "Hello Zoe. It's Alan. Remember me, from the consignment store? You seemed so nice I thought it might be fun to get together for a cup of coffee. Let me know."

All of Alan's messages were similarly friendly. He offered to meet for coffee, for lunch, for a walk in the park. It sounded innocent enough, and certainly his persistence was flattering. But one thing troubled Zoe: How had Alan gotten her last name and phone number? That discomfort—call it a gut feeling—was what kept her from returning any of Alan's calls.

Seeking to put her mind at rest, Zoe called the consignment store, whose owner said she'd seen the man in question before and that he occasionally would buy a shirt from her. She described him as a friendly sort, and she did recall that she had seen him on occasion engage women in conversation. The owner denied, however, ever giving out any customer's name or phone number. Then it occurred to Zoe in a flash: her checking account! Alan must have seen her name—and maybe her address and phone number—on her check!

Zoe's next call was to Alan. She was glad when his voice mail picked up instead of him. She left him a very brief message: "Alan, this is Zoe. I've gotten your messages. I am not interested in getting together with you. Please do not call me again or I will have to report you to the police for harassment."

Zoe had good instincts, and she trusted them. I should also say that she had healthy self-esteem, liked her work, had close friends, and was not experiencing much pressure to find Mr. Right at that time in her life. It may well be that women who are vulnerable for one reason or another— insecure, anxious about being alone, and so on—may have the same instincts but be tempted to ignore them. In Zoe's case, I suspected that Alan (if that was his real name) was cruising consignment shops looking for vulnerable women. Maybe his targets were women who shopped there because they were financially strapped. His behavior was typically predatory. He had identified a target that he thought was vulnerable, and through his phone calls he began stalking his prey.

Fortunately, this story has a happy ending because Zoe trusted her gut feeling and pulled the plug early, instead of accepting Alan's offers.

Assessing Predators: The Predator Inventory

At this point you might find yourself wondering if that man you're dating (or thinking about dating) is a predator. Perhaps you've noticed a few traits in his personality that remind you of the description of the predator given earlier. Maybe you're thinking: Should I just walk away, while I still can?

Before you can make that decision, you need to determine just how well his personality meets the criteria for being a predator. Simply being aggressive, for example, doesn't necessarily mean that a man is predatory. There are other conditions that have to be met, such as being unable to empathize with how you may feel as a result of his being aggressive.

The purpose of the Predator Inventory that follows is to help you make this decision. On the one hand, it is possible that mild tendencies that seem to suggest a predatory nature may be able to be changed. On the other hand, the true predator is to be avoided, period.

Instructions

Each of the following statements describes a personality trait. Rate the man you are interested in on each of these traits, from 0 (not at all) to 10 (totally). When you are finished, total up your ratings to come up with a Predator Index.

1. Has little regard for the rules that most people believe they should follow.   0 1 2 3 4 5 6 7 8 9 10
2. Doesn't take no for an answer.   0 1 2 3 4 5 6 7 8 9 10
3. Will lie or withhold the truth in order to get what he wants.   0 1 2 3 4 5 6 7 8 9 10
4. Is aggressive in getting what he wants.   0 1 2 3 4 5 6 7 8 9 10
5. Shows no remorse for any pain or anxiety he may inflict on others.   0 1 2 3 4 5 6 7 8 9 10
6. Believes that people who get taken advantage of deserve it.   0 1 2 3 4 5 6 7 8 9 10
7. Would steal if he believed he could get away with it.   0 1 2 3 4 5 6 7 8 9 10
8. Would purchase something he knew was stolen.   0 1 2 3 4 5 6 7 8 9 10
9. Does not hesitate to use intimidation when denied what he wants.   0 1 2 3 4 5 6 7 8 9 10
10. Takes advantage of others' weaknesses.   0 1 2 3 4 5 6 7 8 9 10

Predator Index: ____

What Do I Do Now?

You now have your best estimate of just how predatory that man you're interested in may be. If his Predator Index is low (25 or less) and his scores on all of the other inventories you previously completed were also on the low side, you may indeed have a keeper!

But what if this man scores somewhere between 25 and 50? What should you be doing? First, apply the four critical tests for relationships presented in Part Three. See how he stacks up in those four tests. If he passes them all, then it's possible you are dealing with a man who is aggressive in his approach to life, who is willing to bend the rules at times, and who is persistent in getting what he wants. If you are not an assertive woman who also speaks her mind, who knows what she wants, and who can persist in getting what she wants, then you could find yourself getting steamrolled in a relationship with this kind of man. You need to think twice about whether you are ready and willing to go head to head with this man at times in order to reach compromises you can live with.

In contrast, if you are an assertive woman who has no problem persisting in getting what you want, then you may decide to go ahead in the knowledge that this is likely to be an enjoyable but lively relationship. Part Four includes more helpful advice about what to do (and not do) in that kind of relationship.

If the man you are interested in either fails two or more of the critical tests or has a Predator Index higher than 50, my advice is to think long and hard about whether to pursue this relationship. Don't deceive yourself. You have a better-than-50-percent chance of being taken advantage of in one way or another in a relationship with this man. Maybe you've already experienced this but haven't put a label on it. Now you have a label that fits: predator. Your best course of action is, unfortunately, not a pleasant one. What you need to do is either run the other way (if you're not yet in too deep) or cut your losses while you can, and move on with your life.

Know Thyself

We all have vulnerabilities. No one has perfect self-esteem, or is happy about each and every aspect of themselves and their lives. If you want to avoid becoming the victim of a predator, as happened to Jennifer, the best place to begin is by admitting to yourself what your vulnerabilities are. What insecurities do you have that someone could take advantage of to influence you—for example, through flattery? What unrealized dreams or hopes could they play on by making false promises of things to come? Knowing yourself—your strengths and assets as well as your vulnerabilities—is like buying an insurance policy against victimization.

Critical Tests for Relationships

The four chapters in this part of the book describe four tests that you can use to screen out problem men from potential keepers.

The various inventories and indexes you read about in Part Two were a good first step in this process, and in some cases you may have already made a decision to cut your losses and move on. That would be the case if a man scored very high on one of the scales and you concluded that he was indeed highly insecure or narcissistic, for example.

However, many men may fall somewhere in the middle range on one or more of those scales. A man may seem *somewhat* insecure, for example, or be *somewhat* of a beach boy. What do you do then? Is he worth your valuable time and effort? Should you take the chance and devote, perhaps, a year or more of your life to seeing if you can work out a satisfying relationship with him? The critical tests that follow should help you make that decision.

Chapter Twelve

Critical Test #1
Empathy

Empathy refers to the ability to identify with how someone else is feeling and to experience that feeling yourself. For example, empathetic people will feel happy if someone close to them expresses feelings of happiness. They are capable of experiencing the joy that comes from making someone else happy.

By the same token, if someone close to them experiences a loss, empathetic people will identify with that person's grief and experience it as well.

Sometimes, women are fooled into thinking they've found a good man because, they say, "He's in touch with his feelings." Well, the truth is that the narcissist, the insecure man, the beach boy, and even the predator can all be in touch with their feelings. They know when they are happy, sad, angry, or lonely. They know what they want, and what makes them feel good. But life for these men is *all about themselves*. That's the problem. Not only are these men in touch with their feelings, but they expect you to respond to them and meet all their needs. This does not mean, however, that these men are necessarily empathetic—that they can identify with and feel what *you* are feeling.

Valuing Empathy

Empathy plays a crucial role in controlling human behavior. Empathy is one basis for generosity. As already mentioned, the empathetic person can experience the joy of giving. But empathetic people are also able to identify with any pain, fear, or sadness that someone else is experiencing. Moreover, they are able to "connect the dots" in the event that fear, pain, or sadness was caused by something they did (or failed to do).

This ability to empathize is what inhibits us from just going through life doing whatever we want, without regard for others. It is what makes compromise in a relationship possible. If I realize that something I've done has hurt you, because I can empathize with your pain, I will hesitate to do that again, unless I have taken your feelings into account and decided I needed to take that action anyway. However, if I have no idea how my behavior affects you, I'll just keep repeating it. The person who doesn't empathize does whatever he wants to do, regardless of how that makes others feel.

In some cases, an extreme lack of empathy accounts for some pretty nasty behavior. The husband who repeatedly assaults his wife, for example, typically does so in part because he does not identify with the pain he is causing. Instead of acknowledging his own violent personality, he is apt to blame his wife for provoking him. The pedophile who molests young children similarly does not empathize with their fear or pain and is likely to regard them as seductive. The same is true for the rapist, the burglar, and the con artist. It is the inability to identify with how others are feeling that allows men like this to continue to engage in their reprehensible behavior.

Whose Feelings is He in Touch with?

As you become better at getting in tune with a man's feelings, keep your eye out for whether he does the same for you. Does he seem to recognize when you are happy or sad? Does he seem to care if you are upset? Or does he seem to be too preoccupied with his own feelings to notice yours?

Measuring Empathy

Not many men you meet will have an inability to empathize so severe as to put him at risk of being a rapist or a pedophile. The ability to empathize does not appear to be an all-or-nothing phenomenon. At the same time, it is very important that a man have a considerable ability to empathize if you hope to have a successful and fulfilling relationship with him.

Your goal in applying this first critical test for relationships is to decide if the man you are interested in is empathetic enough to be able to sustain a two-way relationship. This will be a subjective decision, to be sure, but the most important thing is to decide whether or not he is sensitive enough for you.

To begin, answer the following questions as they apply to this man:

- Does he seem oblivious (completely unaware) of it when you are feeling sad, frustrated, or angry?
  ___Always
  ___Often
  ___Seldom
  ___Never

- Does he act surprised if you tell him that you are feeling angry or sad?
  ___Always
  ___Often
  ___Seldom
  ___Never

- Does it strike you that he doesn't smile or otherwise acknowledge that he knows when you are feeling happy or excited?
  ___Always
  ___Often
  ___Seldom
  ___Never

- Do you find yourself having to tell him what you are feeling, instead of him knowing it from the way you act?
  ___Always
  ___Often
  ___Seldom
  ___Never

- Is he too much into his own feelings to know what you are feeling?
  ___Always
  ___Often
  ___Seldom
  ___Never

I'm not sure you could make the case that anyone is perfectly empathetic—able to accurately tell what others are feeling all the time. Even in the best relationships there are bound to be times when one partner misses the boat in terms of what the other is feeling. However, in a good relationship, most—if not all—of your answers to these questions should be "seldom" or "never."

If you answered "often" or "always" to two or more questions, go back and look at the indexes you came up with for the six types of problem men described in Part Two. Are any of these scores higher than 50? If not, then it's possible you are simply underestimating this man's ability to empathize.

However, if he had a fairly high score on one of those inventories, your answers to these questions suggest you may have a problem. If you are not already too involved with this man, you should consider getting out now. If you are involved and are hesitant to leave the relationship, the following suggestions might help you make a decision.

Testing For A Man's Capacity to Empathize

There is a way to see if a man is able to empathize and also to see if his capacity to empathize can be strengthened. To do this, you need to be willing to tell this man what you are feeling. You can't just sit back and wait to see if he is sensitive to how you are feeling. Also, you will need to share your feelings, not just once but several times. Finally, you will need to share a range of emotions. Don't just tell him when you are feeling angry, for example, but also let him know when you are feeling any of the following:

- Happy
- Excited
- Sad
- Frustrated
- Lonely

It is important to check out a man's reaction to all of these feelings, because it is possible that he simply has a hard time dealing with one or two of them. Some men, for instance, have difficulty dealing with someone being angry with them, so they block out that emotion. If you make a judgment based only on anger, this man may appear to lack the ability to empathize, when in truth, it's only anger he avoids identifying with. He may be very much capable of empathizing with you when you feel joy or excitement.

Again, to use this technique effectively, you will need to be very clear about what you are feeling. State it directly, when you think you have his attention. Say something like, "I felt _____ all day today," or "I'm feeling _____." Just fill in the blanks with whatever emotion applies.

As you experiment with communicating your feelings directly, you can find out how this man reacts by answering the following questions.

- Does he act indifferent (as if he doesn't really care) if you feel sad, frustrated, or disappointed?
- Does he not respond at all, as if he didn't hear you?
- Does he quickly change the subject from what you are feeling to something else?
- Does he act as if he is impatient with you for telling him how you feel?
- If you share a negative feeling (lonely, sad, frustrated, etc.), does he act irritated?
- Is his response to a negative feeling that you should just "snap out of it" and not "burden" him with such feelings?

If his reactions emerge as a pattern, you need to proceed with extreme caution. You may very well be heading down an emotional one-way street into a relationship in which you are empathetic with this man and respond to his feelings and needs, but he does not do the same for you. In the long run, there is a distinct chance that a relationship with this kind of man will leave you feeling drained, empty, and deeply unhappy.

However, you may discover that it is only certain emotions that this man seems uncomfortable with. In that case, there is some hope that he can, over time, become more empathetic.

Case Study

Sharon and James: Burned Out on Responsibility

Sharon had been dating James for well over a year. She decided to invest herself in this relationship because she found James to be a kind man who was emotionally, financially, and socially stable. She believed that the prospects for a satisfying long-term relationship with him were good. He had good relationships with friends, was educated, had a good job, and shared some of Sharon's interests, such as cross-country skiing and antique hunting.

There was, however, one thing about James that distinctly bothered Sharon. It had to do with how he reacted whenever she would share certain emotions with him. In particular, whenever they would be talking and she would say she was feeling frustrated, disappointed, or sad about something, he would react as if he'd touched a hot flame. In an instant, he would change the subject. This didn't seem to happen, however, when Sharon expressed positive emotions. At such times, James seemed perfectly comfortable with Sharon's happiness. Similarly, he seemed to appreciate her excitement when she would tell him about an interesting antique she'd spotted at a bargain price on eBay.

Sharon's Response

At first, Sharon tried to ignore James's avoidance of negative feelings. She tried telling herself that everyone has foibles, and that this was just one that James happened to have. It didn't seem to interfere with their ability to get along, to make plans, or to have a good time together. However, try as she might to let it go, Sharon found herself becoming increasingly annoyed. It occurred to her that maybe James only wanted to hear good news. In that case, since every relationship was bound to hit some bumps in the road, she could foresee problems ahead. She was not an unhappy person, but at those times when she needed to vent her sadness or pain, she would want to be with someone who could listen, identify with what she was feeling, and comfort her.

Sharon finally confronted James with her frustration and her observation. She did this as gently as she could, while not allowing him to simply avoid discussing her concerns. It was then that she learned something very important about James, which had to do with the role he played as the oldest of five children in a family for whom making ends meet had not always been easy.

An Emotional Fireman

As James described them, his parents were prone to overreacting to even the most minor problems that inevitably occur in a family with limited resources. Perhaps it was because he was the oldest and a responsible child, but starting when he was a youngster, James took it as his responsibility to try to soothe his parents whenever they would become emotionally worked up or to help them find ways around the minor financial crises that cropped up on a regular basis.

James described his role in the family as that of a *fireman*. "It seemed I was always putting out some kind of emotional fire," he explained to Sharon. "Either two people in the family were mad at each other, or one of my siblings did something to get my parents upset, or we had to figure out a way to both pay for food and have the car repaired that week."

To make matters worse, James had transferred the role he played in his family into an unsuccessful marriage. In the latter case, though, he found that he was not really able to put out many fires. His ex-wife had apparently been a very insecure woman who saw herself as a victim. She would constantly complain about being treated unfairly. James would listen, feel badly for her, and then try to make suggestions for how she could resolve her complaint. However, she would always find a reason to reject any suggestion he made. Eventually James concluded that his wife just wanted to complain and didn't really want to resolve any of her complaints, and after a while he found himself tuning out when his wife would begin complaining. Or he would try to change the subject so he didn't have to listen to her go on and on. In time, this turned into a habit, which James brought into his relationship with Sharon.

Once Sharon and James understood what had been going on between them, the door to change was opened. As it turned out, James was not a man who lacked empathy. On the contrary, he was a sensitive man who was burned out on being empathetic because doing so had been very frustrating. He had to admit that Sharon was nothing like either his parents or his ex-wife. She was not looking for James to solve all her problems; rather, she was simply looking for a sympathetic ear—something we all need now and then.

Knowing what was really going on, Sharon once again found herself feeling very hopeful about the future of her relationship with James. She decided she would periodically reassure him that she was only seeking empathy, not a fireman, when she wanted to talk.

Make a Decision

After reading the discussion of empathy and the story of Sharon and James, you need to make a decision. Don't avoid the issue—for example, by telling yourself it's not really important. You can decide for yourself if the relationship you are in passes this first critical test for relationships. If it does, great! If he falls short, though, is it severely so, or not so much? If you believe the latter might be the case, then I recommend that you follow Sharon's example: Get the issue out into the open. See how this man in your life reacts to your observations about him. Try sharing your feelings in a straightforward manner, and then see if he is able to identify with them.

Chapter Thirteen

Critical Test #2 Reciprocity

The second critical test for relationships has to do with reciprocity, meaning the capacity to both give and receive. Reciprocity is as important to a satisfying long-term relationship as the capacity to empathize. After reviewing the various scores that you have come up with for the six different types of problem men described in Part Two, apply this material on reciprocity to the man you are interested in to see how he measures up.

Women who are inclined to be caretakers in their professional lives, personal lives, or both are most vulnerable to minimizing the importance of reciprocity in a relationship. They are more likely than most to find themselves in a relationship in which they give much more than they get. Do you see yourself as a caretaker? If so, the material here will be particularly relevant to you.

Case Study

Ashley and Kobe: A Trail of One-Way Streets

Ashley had won three Teacher of the Year awards for her work as an elementary special-education teacher. Although her professional life was going gangbusters, her personal life was, in her words, "just busters." She had a series of relationships in which she ended up either totally supporting a man who couldn't hold down a job for long or else doing just about everything to maintain a household, from cooking to cleaning to shopping, while also trying to meet a man's need for sex, affection, and attention.

At 36, she was beginning to feel a bit discouraged about the prospects of finding a good man that she could have a family with, without having to carry the entire burden on her shoulders. She wasn't looking for a man to support her, she said, but neither was she looking for a man that she had to support. She had come to think of herself as a magnet for dependent, self-centered men.

Ashley did not want another insecure man, so Kobe was a nice change. However, what she ended up with was an apparent narcissist.

"For Kobe," Ashley said, "life was all about Kobe. I don't know why it took me nearly a year to see that. But I never seem to see things like that when I first get involved."

The Narcissist and the Giver

Like many narcissists, Kobe could be charming. He knew how to dress, how to eat well, and how to have fun. He was intelligent, and unlike some of the men Ashley had gotten involved with, Kobe had at least held down a respectable job for 10 years. However, being the caregiver, for whom life was "all about others," Ashley had something of a blind spot when it came to reciprocity in relationships. She enjoyed the pleasure of giving and found great satisfaction in helping others. These qualities naturally contributed to her excellence in the classroom. Every year, for example, she would spend a couple hundred dollars of her own money on treats and small rewards for her students. She used these not just for the grades a student might earn, but also to acknowledge such qualities as being persistent, being conscientious, and being a "responsible citizen." As a result, her classes were known for their camaraderie and cohesiveness.

In her relationships, including friends, family, and the man in her life, Ashley was similarly thoughtful and giving. She did not shower the people she cared about with extravagant gifts. Instead, she took pleasure in surprising them with small things. She knew what would please the important people in her life and enjoyed making them happy. She'd done this with Kobe, just as she had with the men who had gone before him. As is typical of caretakers, however, Ashley did not often communicate her own needs or have expectations that others should go out of their way to please her. As a teacher, this made sense. Ashley did not expect her students to give her rewards or to praise her. She could tell they liked and respected her, and that was enough for her.

The Waiting Game

As had been the case in her previous relationships, it took a while for Ashley to realize that she was on yet another one-way street. Kobe never went out of his way to do the kinds of things for her that she regularly did for him. She just didn't seem to be on his mind. Ashley realized this, but as she had done before, she let it go. When her birthday rolled around and he forgot it, she got upset. Kobe apologized, but his apology struck Ashley as hollow, designed to placate her. She realized then that waiting for Kobe to do something to please her was not likely to be a winning strategy. Still, she was reticent to come out and ask him to do things—"Buy me some flowers," or "Bring home a special dessert you know I like." It was just not in her nature to be that forward.

So Ashley found herself waiting. And waiting. As you might guess, it took a while, but eventually she started feeling resentful. Her resentment, in turn, made her hold back on being as giving with Kobe as she had been. He definitely took notice of this. He responded by teasing her, saying, "I guess the honeymoon is over," and commenting that Ashley had become complacent in the relationship. At one point, he implied that he might leave if she didn't start treating him better.

Finally, Ashley confronted Kobe with her perception that, contrary to her taking him for granted, he was the one who'd been complacent in the relationship since the beginning.

It was at that point that Ashley more or less woke up to the reality of her relationship with Kobe. It was, she had to admit to herself, yet another one-way street that she was on, and she broke off the relationship with Kobe.

Thinking that she was doomed to such frustrating relationships, Ashley decided to seek out therapy. She wanted a counselor to use as a sounding board, to be able to talk to someone objective the next time she met a man she liked. "I need someone who will be able to see into my blind spot," she said, "and tell me if I'm heading down another one-way street. I can never seem to decide that for myself until I'm well down the street."

Measuring Reciprocity

As a way of gauging just how much someone is able to bring reciprocity into a relationship, respond to the following statements as they apply to a man you are currently either in a relationship with or are contemplating getting involved with.

- He knows what you like (your tastes) when it comes to music, food, clothing, etc.
  ___ Very much
  ___ Somewhat
  ___ Not at all

- He is willing to compromise or take turns, with the result that each of you gets something of what you want.
  ___ Often
  ___ Sometimes
  ___ Rarely or never

- He does little things that he knows will make you feel good.
  ___ Often
  ___ Sometimes
  ___ Rarely or never

- He is willing to go out of his way for you.
  ___ Often
  ___ Sometimes
  ___ Rarely or never

- He would do something you asked him to do, even if it is not something he would choose to do.
  ___ Definitely
  ___ Maybe
  ___ Probably not

Based on the above information about reciprocity, you can probably see just how important this quality is to a good relationship. You also have the tools needed to assess how capable a man is of reciprocity. Keep in mind that the less capable he is, the more likely it is that the relationship is (or will become) a one-way street on which all or most of the compromise and giving is going in one direction—from you to him. This may not bother you much at first, but sooner or later, you will feel resentful and experience a desire to hold back.

Testing for Reciprocity

There is a way for you to see if a man you are interested in is capable of reciprocity and may therefore be a potential keeper. It is based on two simple notions. The first is the idea that each of us has some particular interests, commitments, and connections that we either want to maintain or else feel obligated to maintain. These can include relationships with friends and family, professional obligations, and religious commitments. The second is the idea, as illustrated by Ashley's story, that doing things simply to please someone you care about is an integral part of loving.

The first important measure of a relationship is the ability of each partner to respect the other's commitments and interests, along with the willingness to honor them in a reciprocal way. In a good relationship, therefore, each partner will do the following:

- Be willing to do something they would not otherwise choose to do on their own, in the interest of pleasing the other person.
- Accommodate and even encourage each other's special interests and goals.

The second measure of a good relationship is found in an attitude of give-and-take—a "you scratch my back and I'll scratch yours" approach to being together. That was the kind of reciprocity that Ashley was capable of, but that appeared to be missing from Kobe's personality. In a good relationship, each partner will demonstrate concern for the other person in these ways:

- Do little things to please the other person, for the sheer sake of making them happy.
- Make an effort to learn what pleases the other person, and what their personal tastes are, and take these into account—for example, when choosing gifts.

Case Study

Colleen and Jon: A Failing Grade on the Reciprocity Test

Colleen, who had been dating Jon for about six months, found him to be funny and a pleasure to talk to. They had similar tastes in food, films, and music, and she was beginning to think that this relationship might evolve into something permanent. She was presented with the opportunity to check out the issue of reciprocity when Jon called to say that he needed to attend a corporate training-and-recognition function that was to be held over a weekend in the corporation's home city. Jon asked Colleen to come along as a favor, since all the other people being recognized would be bringing either their spouses or their significant others.

The city where Jon's corporate event would take place held no particular appeal for Colleen. She had some experience with these kinds of corporate events and knew they were typically not much fun. She knew that her role there would be to look good and make a good impression, but not to stand out or do anything to take attention away from Jon. Between the formal corporate meetings and mandatory social events, there would be precious little private time for her and Jon. But she agreed to go anyway, mostly because Jon asked her to. She didn't feel that this was an especially onerous sacrifice on her part.

About a month after Jon's business weekend, Colleen invited him to attend the wedding of one of her nieces. Colleen was not especially close to this niece, who lived several hours away and tended to avoid family gatherings; however, Colleen knew it would be clearly taken as an insult by her sister were she not to go.

When Colleen asked Jon if he would go with her to the wedding, she was taken aback by his quick response. "No thanks," he said. "That doesn't sound like something I'd want to do. Besides, my golfing foursome starts that day."

Is Jon a keeper? You decide. He failed this simple reciprocity test. Skipping his golf game to attend a wedding with Colleen was too much of a sacrifice for him. He had expectations that she should accommodate him, but not that, in the interest of the relationship, he should reciprocate and accommodate her.

In this case Colleen could try telling herself that Jon's reaction was just a fluke: that he really did have the capacity to reciprocate. If she did that, then she would need to try the reciprocity test again. More likely, though, this one experience would foreshadow what this relationship would continue to be like in the future, if she chose to stick with it.

Don't Wait Too Long!

If the man you are interested in truly seems to lack much capacity for reciprocity, don't waste a lot of your time hoping that he will spontaneously change. Instead, consider your abilities to compromise and to give without strings attached as a gift that is best bestowed on a man who also possesses these qualities.

Chapter Fourteen

Critical Test #3
Generosity

In a way, generosity is related to reciprocity, in that both have to do with the capacity to give. Reciprocity, though, is more specific. It has to do with bringing a give-and-take attitude into a relationship. Generosity, by contrast, has more to do with the willingness to give with no strings attached.

True generosity has nothing to do with being flamboyant or extravagant, qualities that are usually intended to impress. Nor does true generosity mean giving with an expectation of getting something in return. I call the latter "Godfather generosity," after the character Don Vito Corleone in *The Godfather* films. Don Corleone could be generous with favors, but there was always an expectation that the recipient of his largesse would eventually be asked to do something in return and would not be free to refuse. This is not the kind of generosity you need to look for in a man who will be a keeper.

Don't Think Only in Terms of Gifts or Money

Generosity can include giving people you care about gifts or money with no expectation of getting anything in return other than the pleasure of pleasing them. However, it is also very possible to express generosity in the following areas:

• Attention
• Affection
• Support and encouragement

In assessing a man's capacity for generosity, it is useful to think in terms of these areas also, not only in terms of the gift-giving form of generosity.

Defining the Generous Personality

In assessing a man's capacity to be generous, you need to look at his ability to be generous not only with you, but also with others he truly loves, such as his children, family, and friends. The truly generous individual tends to bestow his generosity broadly. This does not mean that he is a spendthrift or an extravagant spender. Rather, the generous man gives within his means and does not limit his generosity to material things. He is capable of being generous with his time and attention, for example. He may be willing to help you in a time of need. His primary motivation is the sheer joy or comfort that generosity instills in those who are on its receiving end. This is very different from the kind of pseudo generosity that is motivated by a desire to impress, but that otherwise seems out of character.

Following is a list of qualities that define the truly generous individual.

Believes What's Mine is Yours

The truly generous individual tends not to be highly possessive. He is willing to share what he has. That's not to say he gives away everything he owns. However, he does not hoard the things he owns. This is especially true in his closest relationships. The opposite of generosity is selfishness, which can be summed up in the attitude of "What's mine is mine."

Demonstrates Altruism

Another mark of the generous man is that he cares about the welfare of others—both those he loves and people in general. In contrast to the narcissist, life for the generous man is not just about him. He may, for example, contribute money or time to charities, he may be a mentor to others who are in need of guidance, or he may "adopt" a needy child from another country, whom he will never meet but whose life he will touch. One man I knew, a dentist, contributed untold unpaid hours to help autistic children overcome their fears in order to get the dental care they needed. This required the sort of infinite patience and time that would never be reimbursed by an insurer. These kinds of activities are examples of the altruism that emerges from the heart of the generous person.

Gives to Give, Doesn't Give to Get

In another form of pseudo generosity, a man buys you a gift that he would really like. For example, he buys you a flat-screen television for your birthday, when you know very well that he wants it for himself. Or, there's the old joke about the man who buys his wife a convertible sports car:

"Once it's in the driveway," the joke goes, "it's yours as much as it's hers." A variation of giving-to-get is the man who tells you that he's getting you something and then basically comes out and tells you what he expects you to buy him in return. The generous person will buy you something he knows you will like, with no thought about whether it will benefit him as well, and with no expectation that you will respond in kind.

Case Study

Connie and Eric: Confronting Contingency

Connie had been married to Eric for three years before she finally came to the conclusion that he was a man who didn't seem to have a generous bone in his body. Even back when they were dating, she noticed a decided tendency in him to be possessive when it came to his belongings. One time when she'd been visiting Eric in his condo and it began raining hard, she asked to borrow an umbrella. She could still recall the pained expression that came over his face before he handed it to her. The next day, he left a message on her voice mail reminding her to return the umbrella.

Eric, Connie soon discovered, was the same way about virtually everything he owned. She decided to tolerate this little annoyance, however, since he was also an honest, hard-working, and responsible man. She thought these qualities compensated for his somewhat possessive, miserly ways. She believed she understood where these qualities came from. Eric was the youngest of five children and was pretty much relegated to hand-me-down status in his family. His parents rarely bought him anything new, and even then they would be inclined to look only at those items that were on the clearance tables. The few new things that Eric did own were always subject to being taken without permission by his siblings. So Eric grew up to be a man who safeguarded and was possessive about his things.

While Connie found it in her heart to accept Eric's tendency to be possessive and stingy, she had a much harder time with the way he always made giving contingent. For instance, when Connie's birthday would approach, Eric would bring up the issue of what she wanted as a gift. But he would do this in a peculiar—and for Connie, annoying—way. He would talk not just about what she might want for her birthday, but what he might want for his. Connie couldn't help but notice that whatever she said she wanted would be matched by something of comparable value that Eric wanted. In other words, if Connie asked for something she knew was fairly expensive, she could count on Eric talking about wanting something of equal value when his birthday came around.

What Connie found objectionable about Eric's contingent approach to gift-giving was not that he might want something expensive in return for buying her something expensive. She was really okay with that. What bothered Connie, rather, was her perception that Eric did not seem to believe that she was capable of being generous at all unless he gave her something first. He apparently had little faith that she would ever give him something nice unless he gave her something nice, and unless he let her know that he expected things to work that way.

Connie figured that Eric's contingent approach also had its roots in his early experiences in his family, but she found this trait harder to tolerate than his possessiveness or stinginess. That was because it was an affront to her basically generous nature. When she finally could take it no more and confronted him, Eric seemed genuinely surprised. Making giving contingent on receiving something in return had been so ingrained in his personality for so long that he was oblivious to how it might make another person feel. Clearly embarrassed, he apologized to Connie.

That confrontation turned out to be an eye-opener that allowed Eric to move a little toward becoming a more generous man. It did not transform his personality; however, he did drop his habit of making gift-giving a tit-for-tat experience. When he asked Connie what she wanted, for example, for Christmas or her birthday, he no longer talked about what he might want in return. And on a couple of occasions he bought her small gifts for no special reason.

Happily, when Eric exhibited these changes, Connie was able to drop the resentment that had been building in her. She appreciated the fact that Eric was open to self-examination and was willing to make an effort to change in order to please her. And she believed that the changes he made increased the prospects for a happy future for the two of them.

Assessing Generosity

In addition to reflecting on the previous material, your reponses to the following statemetns will help you decide whether a man's personality includes generosity:

- Donates some of his time and/or money to charity.   ___True ___False
- Seems to derive pleasure simply by making someone else happy.   ___True ___False
- Gives through spending time, not just spending money.   ___True ___False
- Is affectionate toward those he cares about.   ___True ___False

- Demonstrates an attitude of "What's mine is yours."   ___True ___False
- Gives without thinking about what he will get
  in return.   ___True ___False
- Cares about people in general.   ___True ___False

It's up to you to decide whether a man you are interested in is generous enough for you to be happy with him. Not everyone is equally generous, and generosity should not be confused with being irresponsible or extravagant. A man who has a high score on any one of the inventories in Part Two, but who also appears to be lacking in generosity, may not be a good prospect for a long-term relationship. In such a relationship, you will most likely have to ask for the things you want and persevere to get them. On the one hand, if you prefer a man who puts effort into learning what you like and who does things to make you happy without your having to ask, then you will probably be unhappy with a relatively ungenerous man. On the other hand, if you don't mind asking and pushing for what you want, then you might be okay with that kind of man, depending on just how ungenerous he is.

Another factor to consider in deciding whether a man is a keeper is your own personality. How generous do you see yourself as being? Your best bet is to find a match between yourself and a man in terms of generosity. If you are a generous person, you will probably discover that an ungenerous man will discourage you from doing some of the things you like to do, simply because he will regard giving for its own sake to be a waste of time, money, or both. This, in turn, can lead to a lot of conflict. You'd be better off looking for a relationship with a man who is comfortable with your level of generosity.

Chapter Fifteen

Critical Test #4
Humility

Making a relationship work in the long run requires all of the personal qualities described in this part of the book: empathy, reciprocity, generosity, *and* the subject of this chapter—humility.

No one is a saint, and no man will be perfect with respect to all of these qualities. However, both partners need to be capable of bringing all of these traits to the table if they hope to have a fulfilling relationship that brings out the best in each of them and helps them realize their potential.

In these days of excess and egocentricity, it is easy to mistake arrogance for self-confidence. We seem to be enamored with people who are clearly self-centered and self-absorbed—in other words, narcissistic and arrogant. There is a big difference, though, between self-confidence and arrogance or narcissism. The narcissist may be easy to get along with, but that is contingent on him getting whatever he wants. An arrogant man is certainly self-assured. Fundamentally, however, this man lacks the humility that is necessary to keep self-centeredness from getting out of control.

It is also possible to confuse a man who is humble with a man who has low self-esteem. The insecure man is a perfect example of the man who may, on the surface, appear humble, but who, in fact, suffers from a negative self-image and is prone to feeling inferior.

Defining Humility

The following is a list of personal qualities and traits to look for in order to decide if a man possesses the quality of humility.

Not a Fisherman

A man who is truly humble does not fish for compliments. He may appreciate a compliment, but you do not get the feeling that he is trying to pull compliments out of you. In contrast, a man who seems to need constant affirmation will eventually drain you. In his neediness, he may appeal to your maternal side (if you are a maternal woman by nature).

However, inwardly this man feels inferior and needs to have his ego continually blown up. He is like a balloon with a tiny leak—you may try to keep it inflated, but eventually, you will feel exhausted.

A Balanced Self-Image

The humble individual recognizes his skills, personal assets, and abilities, as well as his limitations and even his liabilities and weaknesses. As you get to know him better, you see that he is aware of a balance in himself between personal assets and liabilities.

No Bragging

The narcissist tends to brag and boast. He's a showboat who is sure to let you know what he owns, how successful and smart he is, and so on. A humble person feels comfortable in his own skin and has no need to puff himself up.

No Comparing

Comparing himself to others is a hallmark of the insecure man. Usually, this comparing takes the form of criticism and fault-finding in order to compensate for his feelings of inferiority. This is not humility; rather, it is low self-esteem.

Team Player

A humble individual is capable of working as a team member to achieve shared goals. He is willing to share in the credit or rewards for success, as well as responsibility for any failures. He does not seek out scapegoats when things don't go well. In his personal life he is ready and willing to divide responsibilities—for example, routine housework and chores, or parenting—so that one person is not carrying an unfair share of the load.

If you think of a marriage as teamwork, then this quality of humility may be the single most important ingredient in a successful marriage. In contrast, the insecure man is threatened by strength and competence in a woman, the narcissist seeks the glory but none of the hard work, and the control freak has to be the boss all the time.

Tolerant

A humble individual is able to accept the fact that others may have opinions that are valid, even though they differ from his own. By the same token, a humble individual is able to accept and respect the fact that others sometimes need to make their own decisions and lead their own lives, even if he would do it differently.

Try Expressing a Different Opinion

Here's a quick and easy test for humility: As you get to know a man, you will no doubt get to know what some of his opinions are about various issues. Since no two people are going to think exactly alike about everything, sooner or later you will probably discover something on which your opinion differs from his. Try sharing that difference and see how he responds. On the one hand, if he seems quite comfortable and tolerant of this difference, take that as a good sign. On the other hand, if he tries to talk you out of your opinion or in any way comes across as critical or judgmental, you would be wise to take note of that and begin looking at all of the other qualities described here.

Case Study

Nadia and Aaron: A Failure of Humility

Aaron was the proverbial self-made man, and as such, was very attractive to many women. He built his own business from the ground up starting at age 18, and although he had relatively little formal education, he was well read and capable of carrying on intelligent conversations across a broad range of topics. In many ways, he cut an imposing figure, yet some of the women who'd fallen for him over the years would have said that Aaron's only fault, ironically, was that he was hyper-competent.

Aaron took pride in the fact that he could take care of himself and was not dependent on others for just about anything he needed. He was the youngest son of a man who, despite being educated, had the misfortune of being laid off as a result of corporate mergers not just once, but three times. Each time the family fell on fairly hard times. Twice they had to relocate when Aaron's father finally found employment in another area of the country. Though his mother worked part-time as a licensed practical nurse, it was Aaron's father's salary as an accountant that the family relied on to pay the lion's share of its living expenses.

In response to his father's misfortunes, Aaron resolved to never be financially dependent on a corporation over which he had no control. At 15, he started his first business, which was mowing and raking lawns. He started out with a second-hand, gas-powered, push lawnmower that he got for free from a kind neighbor who was trading up. By the time he was

17, Aaron was employing four other boys to mow and rake lawns. By then, he owned four mowers, including two riding mowers that could do the work of a push mower in a fifth of the time. He also owned two leaf blowers that were kept constantly busy every fall.

Now 38, Aaron was the owner of a successful landscaping company that did residential and commercial work. Annual revenues were well over a million dollars, and Aaron was secure enough financially that he was considering investing in a medical arts building that was to be constructed on a property for which his company had the landscaping contract.

When Nadia met Aaron, she, like many women before her, was impressed. He was not only intelligent and successful, but handsome and well-mannered. His people skills were evident from their first encounter, at a holiday gathering organized by the construction firm Aaron was thinking about investing with. Nadia's position within that company involved finding suitable tenants for the various building projects it was constructing.

Nadia, who had dated a lot of men, felt she had become expert at sizing them up quickly, and her initial impression of Aaron was that he was a potential keeper. From her own experience, she knew that some men were put off by an assertive and straightforward woman. These attributes proved to be valuable assets in her work, but in relationships they appeared to represent threats, at least to certain men. But Aaron seemed to be quite comfortable with her. She noticed, too, that while he dressed well and drove a nice vehicle, Aaron did not seem to be ostentatious or motivated to impress. So when he called her a few days later and suggested meeting for lunch, she happily accepted.

The Smugness of a Self-Made Man

It wasn't until Nadia had been dating Aaron for a few months that she began to realize that he was not just a self-made man, but a self-sufficient one who definitely had a smug side to him. Initially, she thought this was simply self-confidence. However, as time went on and he gradually revealed more of himself, Nadia began to realize that Aaron was, in fact, arrogant. The first thing she noticed was his attitude toward the people who worked in his landscaping business. What struck Nadia was that, although Aaron had gotten his own start in life by pushing a lawnmower, he had a low opinion of the men and women he now employed to do the same thing. Many of these people were young and, from her point of view, had futures potentially as bright as his. Yet Aaron spoke of them as if they were all unintelligent and lazy. Annoying as this was, it was a trait that Nadia felt she could ignore.

What made Nadia burn, however, was Aaron's apparent disregard for her ideas and opinions. He did not show this in a blatant way (say, by putting her down), but was more subtle (for example, by not responding when she expressed an opinion). It didn't take very long for Nadia to realize that Aaron was not much interested in her opinions about most anything, from what wine to order at dinner, to where would be a good place to take a vacation, to who would make the best next president of the United States.

Then, over dinner one night, Aaron shared his opinion that his father, although a competent accountant, had been a bit of a fool for losing three jobs. Aaron regarded himself as "failure-proof" because he owned his own business. Nadia found this condescending attitude on Aaron's part irritating, since her impression of Aaron's father, though she'd never met him, was that he was a responsible person who always tried to do his best for his family. Her own father had been similarly hard-working, not self-made as Aaron was, and she had loved and respected him for that.

The last straw came when Aaron let Nadia know that he thought selling and renting retail office space was a job that did not require much skill or intelligence. Try as she might to bite her tongue and swallow her pride—she was outspoken herself, a woman who thought she was intelligent and who took pride in her career—Nadia could not let this last insult go by the boards. It was more or less at that moment that she realized that Aaron was not going to be a keeper, at least not for her, after all. As attractive as he was in an objective way—or, as she put it, "on his resume"—she could not imagine being in a relationship for long with a man who was so arrogant. By that time, she had already pretty much stopped talking to Aaron about anything substantial and no longer looked forward to seeing him.

Measuring Humility

Aaron is obviously an example of a man who seriously lacked humility. It's easy to see how difficult it might be to have a satisfying long-term relationship with a man like that. Put another way, you can see what you would have to sacrifice in order to be in a relationship with someone like that. Still, based on first impressions, a man like Aaron can be quite attractive. The key is being able to know what constitutes humility—to be able to discriminate between self-confidence and arrogance.

Your reponses to the following statements about a man you are interested in can help you determine whether he is capable of bringing a measure of humility into a relationship.

- He respects my opinions even when they differ from his.
  - ___ Always
  - ___ Often
  - ___ Sometimes
  - ___ Never

- He is aware of his strengths and abilities, as well as his flaws and weaknesses.
  - ___ Very much
  - ___ Somewhat
  - ___ Very little
  - ___ Not at all

- He is a good team player, willing to share in household responsibilities, and so on.
  - ___ Very much
  - ___ Somewhat
  - ___ Very little
  - ___ Not at all

- He believes he is right.
  - ___ Always
  - ___ Often
  - ___ Sometimes
  - ___ Never

- He is open to advice and suggestions.
  - ___ Always
  - ___ Often
  - ___ Sometimes
  - ___ Never

- He thinks he is better than others.
  - ___ Very much
  - ___ Somewhat
  - ___ A little
  - ___ Not at all

- He is open to compromise.
  - ___ Always
  - ___ Often
  - ___ Sometimes
  - ___ Never

There no doubt are few people who possess humility in the extreme. But it is also true that a good relationship requires a degree of humility on each person's part. The humble man (or woman) is someone who respects differences in taste or opinion, who has a balanced self-image, who can work as part of a team, and who is open to suggestions and is willing to compromise.

If the man you are interested in appears to possess at least a modicum of humility, you are in luck. Assuming he also possesses a modicum of the other qualities described in Part Three, you probably have someone with whom it will be possible to enjoy a fulfilling, long-term relationship.

In contrast, men who do poorly on the humility test will almost always do poorly on one or more of the other critical tests described in Part Three. Depending on just how poorly they do on these critical tests, consider yourself warned in the event you decide to pursue the relationship.

Keeping a Good Man Once You Find Him

Since you are reading this final part of the book, chances are you've decided that the man in your life is worth the investment of your time and energy. He's not perfect (who is?), but hopefully, he does not fit the profile to an extreme degree of any of the problem men described in Part Two. Moreover, he basically has passed the four critical tests for relationships provided in Part Three. All things considered, he appears to be a keeper.

The material in Part Four is intended to tell you what to watch out for, as well as things to do (and not do), in order to avoid playing into a man's faults and inadvertently making them worse. Many such pitfalls are surprisingly easy to slip into. Armed with the information you read here, you should find yourself in a position to help bring out the best, not the worst, in a man.

Chapter Sixteen

Keeping Insecurity in Check

Okay, as best you can tell, the man you've been dating for nearly two years has some signs of insecurity. However, he does not appear to be severely insecure. He also passed Part Three's four critical tests for relationships, if not with flying colors. Another consideration is the fact that you have already invested a lot of time and effort in this relationship, and in that time he hasn't done anything to trigger a warning signal to abandon the relationship.

The worst you can say of this man is that he sometimes needs a lot of reassurance, tends to be critical of himself, seems at times to give up too easily, and has shown occasional flashes of jealousy of other men as well as some envy toward you and what you've accomplished in life.

The bottom line, though, is that he's much better than some of the other men you've been with, and you don't think it would be in your best interest to pull out now. The question then becomes: Are there things you should be doing (and not doing) to help make this relationship work?

It's His Insecurity, Not Yours

As you read through the suggestions that follow, it's important to keep in mind that there may be things you can do, as well as things you can avoid doing, in order to help keep a man's insecurity in check. However, it's equally important to keep in mind that it's *his* insecurity, not yours. You didn't cause it, and you probably can't cure it. He's the only one who may be able to truly get past his insecurity, if he is motivated to do so—and perhaps with the help of a good therapist. All I am talking about here are ways in which you may be able to help your situation by not feeding his insecurity.

Strategies for Living With an Insecure Man

There are definitely things a woman can do that can help in a relationship with an insecure man. There are also a number of things a woman can do that will have the unintended effect of worsening a man's insecurity. Often, women inadvertently make insecurity worse, typically by accommodating it too much (thinking that this will make it go away). It is important that a woman who believes her partner is insecure follow these guidelines.

Reassure Him, Up to a Point

The insecure man can benefit from hearing, on a more-or-less-regular basis, that he is loved and respected. Because he fears abandonment (often unconsciously) and because he also feels inferior to other men on some level, it can be helpful to offer unsolicited reassurance to the effect that you love him and respect him for who he is. Let him know now and then that he can count on you, and that you believe you can count on him. Do not get caught up, though, in thinking that you have to tell him you love him ten times a day.

In a relationship with an insecure man, you need to be aware that withholding reassurance and praise is likely to motivate him to seek it all the more. That, in turn, could potentially stir up some resistance in you. In the end, you could get caught up in a vicious cycle of him pressuring you for praise and reassurance, and you digging your heels in and resisting giving it to him. Heading down that road is something you want to avoid, if possible.

Expect Insecurity from Time to Time

Don't waste your time thinking that his insecurity is simply going to disappear forever—for example, because you love him. On the contrary, expect insecurity to raise its ugly head now and then, especially in the form of jealousy and envy. When he becomes jealous, point out times recently when you've told him (or better yet, showed him) that you love him. Act surprised that he would be jealous of another man.

If he seems to be feeling envious of you, point out something about him that you admire. If at some point he talks about seeking counseling in order to overcome his low self-esteem, encourage him to do so. If you've been in therapy, let him know how it helped you. Don't suggest that he has emotional problems; rather, let him know that you respect a man who is willing to work on improving himself.

Balance Privacy with Openness

It's important to maintain some sense that your relationship includes not only *open* or *shared* space, but a bit of *his* space and a bit of *your* space. In other words, being in a relationship doesn't mean that you should have to totally forfeit your privacy. He should not, for example, be opening your mail (or you his, for that matter). He should not be checking your cell phone log or your e-mail, unless there is some extraordinary reason for doing so. Satisfying his insecurity is not a good enough reason for him to violate your privacy.

Similarly, while you may decide to open a joint checking account from which the household bills are paid, it is a good idea for each of you to maintain modest personal accounts from which you can buy gifts for each other or save up for something you'd like to buy for yourself. You should not feel compelled to account for every dollar you spend.

Insecurity is like a campfire that can easily spread into a forest fire if you don't take pains to keep it in check. Sacrificing all your privacy in order to help an insecure man feel better is like removing the stones that circle a campfire—it's likely to allow the fire to spread. Forcing a man to accept a certain amount of your personal privacy is more likely to help keep his insecurity in check; surrendering all your privacy, in contrast, is likely to only make it worse.

Maintain Your Outside Interests and Commitments

Do not give up your friends or outside interests—especially those you had before you met—even though you may devote somewhat less time to those friends or activities as your relationship grows. Insecurity breeds jealousy. The insecure man may question who you spend your time with, or what you talk about. Consciously or unconsciously, he may fear that letting you out of his sight is dangerous to the relationship. As a result, he may be tempted to ask you to account for every minute of your time when you are not with him. This is just as bad an idea as having to account for every dollar you spend—it will make his insecurity worse, not better. The more you abandon outside interests or friends, the narrower your life will become. That will not make a man's insecurity go away, but it very well may make you feel resentful and depressed.

Don't Become Asexual

Insecure men are notorious for accusing the women in their lives of being intentionally flirtatious or provocative. Suddenly, the way you dressed when he met you, which was apparently fine with him then, becomes offensive to him once you commit to the relationship.

Do not start dressing to avoid sparking jealousy in an insecure man. That's not to say that your wardrobe may not change at all. Chances are that when you were in dating mode, you did dress in ways intended to draw more attention to yourself. However, you most likely also dressed in ways that made you feel good about yourself. Don't stop doing that. You still need to dress in ways that make *you* feel attractive. That's a part of healthy self-esteem. Resist any pressure from him to "dress down," unless you want to do that for yourself, not just because he wants you to.

Case Study

Gina and Frank: A Case of Insecurity Gone Wild

When Gina met Frank, it was obvious to her that one thing he found attractive about her was her looks: her face, the way she dressed, and her figure. She was not naive, and although she realized that he was probably also attracted to other things—her sense of humor, the fact that she was fast on her feet and good with banter, and the fact that she had a good job—physical attraction most definitely played a part in creating the chemistry between them.

With lustrous, auburn hair and big, dark-brown eyes, along with a curvy body, Gina was indeed an attractive woman. She also had a lot of energy and enjoyed the company of a number of women friends, many of whom she'd known for 15 years or longer.

The Years with Joe

Gina had been married once, briefly, when she was 22 years old. She and her ex-husband, Joe, dated steadily for five years, beginning when they were seniors in high school, and though Joe wasn't much of a student, he was talented with his hands and had gone to school to become a carpenter. They'd been drawn to each other, Gina had to admit, in large part by physical attraction. She was as turned on by Joe's rough-hewn good looks and muscular body as he was turned on by her. Gina had imagined Joe as someone who could be counted on to take care of her, who had skills and common sense. She thought Joe would make a good father.

Even though she'd known him for a long time, Gina's decision to marry Joe ultimately had been impulsive. They were at the end of a long-weekend vacation on Cape Cod. It was a beautiful fall day and they were walking along the beach. It had been a romantic weekend indeed, and when Joe, out of the blue, said, "We should get married," Gina said yes. Sadly, it wasn't long after they returned from a brief honeymoon that Gina began to feel uncomfortable.

Why the sudden discomfort? For one thing, Gina had just completed nursing school and was on the brink of a successful career. Joe, meanwhile, had just gotten laid off from a construction job because the contract was finished, and no new work was yet in sight. Right then and there, Gina began to reconsider her fantasy of what life would be like with Joe. Suddenly, as the reality that Joe's work would never be as secure as hers sunk in, the image of security that was so important to Gina seemed shaky. Of course, that in itself was not enough to make her want to leave Joe.

A year into the marriage, Joe got laid off a second time, again for lack of work. Over that same period of time he'd steadily increased his consumption of alcohol; and while he was waiting for new work to come along, he'd developed a habit of meeting some carpenter friends at a local sports bar most afternoons. Six months later, no new work had come along. Meanwhile, Gina was being promoted and was training to be a nurse in a pediatric intensive care unit. The idea of having to support the two of them on her salary was so far off from Gina's dream of what married life would be that she just couldn't keep her disappointment hidden. Soon, her sarcastic side began showing itself, and spats between them, followed by long periods of silence, became more and more frequent. Eventually, Joe decided to call it quits.

Frank: Stable but Self-Critical

When she met Frank, one of the things Gina liked about him was that he was educated and had a stable job as an administrator in a social services agency. Ever since her experience with Joe, a stable job had become important to Gina—more important than rugged looks or a man's ability to fix things. Frank had a good sense of humor, was close to his family, and treated Gina well. So what if he couldn't replace a broken light switch?

In truth, Frank was a fairly insecure man, though he kept his insecurity under wraps as much as he could. Gina didn't really see anything in Frank that bothered her much, until after he had proposed to her and she accepted. Prior to that, the only thing she had noticed was that Frank could be self-critical at times. If something broke when he was trying to fix it, for example, he might lose his temper, mutter to himself about being "stupid," and throw the thing down. He also felt that he was too soft, not muscular enough, even though Gina told him several times that he was not fat, was in good shape, and was attractive, even if he didn't have a six-pack for a stomach.

The first signs of insecurity in Frank appeared about a month after the engagement, when they were going to a party. Just before they were about to leave, Frank looked at Gina and said something like, "Don't you think you look kind of provocative for an engaged woman?"

Gina was thrown off balance. Frank had never said anything like that before. Also, she hadn't dressed any more "provocatively" that evening than she had since she first met Frank. She knew he found her sexually attractive, and she definitely wanted to keep it that way. She was dressing for him and because she liked feeling attractive, not to seduce other men.

Frank's remark led to a brief tiff, but then Gina dropped it. About a month later, Frank made another comment. This time, he suggested that Gina wear a sweater over her blouse before they went out for dinner at their favorite restaurant. She asked him why. He didn't respond, though she knew very well why he wanted her to put on a sweater, and it raised her hackles. She retreated to her bedroom and changed her clothes completely, making sure to take enough time so that they missed their reservation and had to sit in the bar for half an hour waiting for a table to become available. Their conversation over dinner was sparse and tense.

The final straw for Gina came when she met a couple of girlfriends after work one night for drinks. This was something she'd been doing about once a month for years, and Frank never commented on it when they were dating. This time, though, he asked whom she was meeting, where they would meet, and when she would get home. They weren't yet living together, and Frank's nosiness bothered Gina. She definitely showed her irritation when she sarcastically gave Frank all the information he asked for. Then, when she got home to find three messages on her voice mail, she called him and chewed him out. "I may be your fiancé," she told him, "but that doesn't mean that you own me."

Fortunately for both of them (and their relationship), Gina confronted Frank's growing insecurity soon after this third incident. She sat Frank down and told him she loved him and wanted to marry him. At the same time, she said, she now knew that he was insecure. His self-criticism and jealousy were sure signs of it. She told Frank that she realized that neither of them was perfect. She could accept his insecurity to a degree, she added. However, she also flatly told him that her belief was that if she gave into his insecurity—dressed the way he wanted her to dress, stopped having the occasional night out with friends—his insecurity would only get worse, not better. Therefore, for the sake of their relationship, she was going to keep her friendships, and she was going to dress the way she'd always dressed. If Frank could not live with that, then he would have to make a decision.

Lessons Learned

In terms of having a successful relationship with an insecure man, Gina was making all the right moves. Of course, it would help if Frank's insecurity was not too severe. It would also help if he decided to seek counseling in order to overcome it.

The truth is that insecurity undermines a man in more areas of life than just his intimate relationships. It can also undermine his success in his career, his friendships, and his ability to be a good parent. So there are many reasons it is a good idea for the insecure man to recognize his insecurity and do something about it.

The most important things Gina did can be summarized as follows.

Name It for What It Is

Gina did not try to call insecurity anything but insecurity. She pointed out its symptoms in Frank, and let him know in a caring but straightforward way that it was going to be a problem. She did not, however, tell him he was mentally ill or suggest that he was in any way an inferior person because he was insecure. You could say that she allowed Frank to retain his dignity despite his insecurity.

Maintain Some Privacy and Personal Space

Gina let Frank know that she was not going to sacrifice her friendships or the little bit of a private life that she had in order to try to make him feel less insecure. She explained that she believed it was important for both of them to maintain their closest friendships, and that this was no reflection on her commitment to him or their relationship. In fact, she explained that she thought of their relationship as a separate, third entity with a life of its own. "There's me, there's you, and there's our relationship," she said to Frank. "All three need some of our time and attention. If we neglect any of them, we can be headed for trouble." Gina's friendships would continue to be a small but important piece of the pie in terms of how she divided her time among her priorities.

Don't Change Who You Are

It goes without saying that the decision to commit ourselves to a relationship requires us to make changes in our lifestyles. We do have obligations to the person we are committing to, as well as to the relationship itself. That said, Gina was right, for example, when she told Frank that she was not willing to change the way she dressed. She did this not to defy him, but because she knew that dressing more conservatively, as he wanted her to do, would not actually help Frank become more secure, but, on the contrary, would most likely only make matters worse between them.

Assess Your Options

As it turned out, Gina successfully nipped insecurity in the bud. The last time I heard from her, she and Frank were doing well. They had just celebrated their third anniversary, and from her point of view, the third entity—their relationship—was "thriving."

You, too, may be able to have a successful relationship even if the man in your life is a little insecure. In order to do so, however, you may have to borrow a page from Gina's book and have the courage to face insecurity and not give in to it.

Chapter Seventeen

Striving for Balance with a Narcissist

The idea of living with a narcissist may strike you as silly. "Why would anyone want to do that?" you might ask. Well, the truth is that there are many degrees of narcissism. To be sure, a man who is severely narcissistic is not likely to be a keeper. That kind of man may not be worth investing your valuable time and energy in, especially if you think you're somehow going to change him or that he will voluntarily give up his narcissism out of love for you.

However, a man may fall somewhere in the middle on the Narcissism Inventory. In addition, although he may not have had perfect scores on them, he may basically have passed the four critical tests for relationships. In that case, you may decide that this is a relationship worth pursuing. Once again, the question becomes: What should I do, and not do, in order to help make this relationship work in the long run?

It Should Be at Least a Little About You

A little narcissism is not necessarily a bad thing. If you find yourself often being a doormat in relationships, or if you feel that others get a lot more of what they want than you do, you might benefit from professional counseling. The goal of that counseling should be, first, to find out why your expectations are so low. Maybe you feel it's selfish to expect very much. Or maybe you feel underentitled because you didn't get very much of what you wanted when you were growing up. Once you have some idea about the roots of your low expectations, you should use your counselor as a coach who can help you to raise your expectations and feel good about doing so, and also to assert yourself so that you get more of what you want. Don't worry—this will not turn you into a narcissist. However, it could be enormously helpful if you find yourself in a relationship with a man who tends to be narcissistic.

Alice and Jeremy: It's All About Him–Or Is It?

A little narcissism, one could argue, is not necessarily a bad thing; but if the popular expression "It's all about me" seems to sum up a man's personality, it's a sign of potential trouble ahead. The challenge facing you will be to maintain some balance between life being about him *and* about you. That was precisely the challenge Alice faced in her marriage to Jeremy.

Jeremy was both talented and narcissistic. From the time he was a child, his parents touted his abilities and helped to inflate his ego beyond a healthy level. His father, starting from scratch, built a successful insurance brokerage in a medium-size town in the Midwest. Now retired, he still enjoyed his standing in the community. He was, as they say, a big fish in a small pond, and he loved it.

Jeremy, age 40, was engaged in a successful business career of his own that had already made him, Alice, and their two children financially secure for life. Unlike his father, Jeremy left the small town he grew up in and made it big in the country's financial centers. Even if everything fell apart the next day, he had enough money and securities, real estate, and other investments socked away to make sure, at a minimum, that their house would be secure and their children would be able to go to the best colleges.

Jeremy was well aware of his success, and while he was generous with his family, he also did not hesitate to reward himself. He had all the toys, and then some. He was quite vocal in asserting his views and opinions, from what house they should buy to where they should go on vacation to what they should do as a family on the weekend. These personality traits had served Jeremy well in the business world, where he had a reputation for being a mover and a shaker, someone who got things done. In the process, he made millions for the companies he worked for and made sure he got his rewards in return.

Alice's Place in the Relationship

Alice's personality was very different. She came from a working-class family that, if not exactly struggling, enjoyed far fewer luxuries than Jeremy did. In addition, Alice had been a "parental" child, helping to raise two younger siblings while her parents held down full-time jobs. In school, she worked hard and had a reputation for being bright and diligent. Her grades were outstanding, and she attended college on a full scholarship. After that, she put herself through law school with a combination of work and loans.

Rather than make a law career her top priority, though, Alice elected to work part-time in order to devote more time to raising her son and daughter. When she did something she was proud of, Alice might reward herself by buying a new sweater. In contrast, when Jeremy achieved a goal he'd set for himself, he might buy himself a new motorcycle or expensive speakers for their home theater system.

The Enabler Becomes Depressed

Alice was grateful for the security Jeremy's success had provided for their family. However, after 14 years of marriage, during which time they'd relocated four times as he moved ever higher up the corporate ladder, she was feeling depressed—so depressed, in fact, that she began to think about divorce. She toyed with ideas about how they might co-parent the children, and what she would do in her "time off."

When Alice revealed what she had been thinking to Jeremy during one of her darker moments, he panicked. That led to a quick appointment with a marriage counselor.

In counseling, Alice was forced to acknowledge that while Jeremy may have a narcissistic streak, she had also enabled this behavior in him by being so modest in her own expectations and so unassertive in their relationship. Faced with no counterbalancing resistance, Jeremy's ego had thrived. Alice had come to feel depressed and resentful of the very egotism that she had helped to promote. Not that she had made her husband a narcissist; but Alice had definitely not done much to balance Jeremy's considerable ego and will with her own. If she chose the path of least resistance and divorced Jeremy, chances are that she would repeat this pattern again in another relationship. Walking away would not help her to break free from her low-expectation, unassertive approach to life.

Alice made a commitment to work with Jeremy and the marriage counselor for six months before considering divorce. The difficulty she encountered in making her needs, goals, and desires more of a priority and asserting herself, especially in the face of Jeremy's assertiveness, was considerable. At times, she told the therapist, it seemed as if she were being asked to remake her personality. In a sense, this was accurate. Yet what were the alternatives? Divorce? Try to find a man who had low expectations and was as unassertive as she was?

One thing that Alice had going for her in her effort to change and salvage her marriage was that, as narcissistic as Jeremy was, he genuinely loved her. He was not so narcissistic that he could not empathize with how his wife felt. He was capable of compromising and was willing to give to others, not just to himself. In time, their combined efforts could well form the basis for a much more mutually fulfilling and exciting marriage.

Strategies for Living With a Narcissist

Here are some dos and don'ts to keep in mind if you decide to pursue (or stay in) a relationship with a man who has clear narcissistic tendencies.

Don't Be Shy

Ponder this: If you are a very shy woman who rarely speaks your mind or asks for what you want, sooner or later you're likely to find yourself in Alice's position, feeling depressed and probably resentful. A narcissistic man may not be a good choice for you. Maybe you secretly admire him for being narcissistic and for getting more of what he wants than you do. But don't think that this will rub off on you. You are better off taking a lesson from Alice and working on your ability to decide what you want, and speak up. If necessary, seek out the help of a therapist who can coach you on determining what you want and setting goals. The biggest challenge you'll face will be raising your expectations (to believe you deserve more) and persisting, rather than giving up easily.

Be Prepared to Use Your Elbows

Have you ever heard people talk about learning to eat meals as a member of a large family—about having to "use your elbows" to be sure you get some food on your plate? Well, that's the best way to approach being in a relationship with a narcissistic man. If you aren't prepared to elbow your way to the table, you might not get much food. Again, it isn't reasonable to expect someone who is self-centered to immediately change gears and start thinking about what you want. The best you can do is assert your needs and desires, and be prepared to keep asserting them in order to get your share of the pie.

Take Care of Yourself

Narcissists don't usually have a hard time doing nice things for themselves. They don't believe they have to wait for a reward or for someone to be nice to them. They are generous with themselves. If you think about it, it might not be such a bad idea to at least occasionally borrow a page from the narcissist's playbook and apply it to yourself. I'm not encouraging you to become a narcissist yourself, but I am encouraging you to make yourself somewhat of a priority. The more you do the opposite—consistently ignore yourself and put others ahead of yourself—the greater the gap will be in your relationship, since the narcissist will continue to take care of himself.

Make sure you budget time and money for clothing, makeup, exercise, visits to the salon, an occasional massage, and so on. It may not be appropriate to pamper yourself every day, but it wouldn't hurt you to do so once in a while.

The man who is not a total narcissist may indeed be capable of thinking about you, at least sometimes, and of being generous. But you should be aware of how generous he is willing to be with himself and match it with generosity toward yourself. For example, make sure that at least some of the ways you reward yourself roughly match the ways in which he rewards himself.

Keep Commitments in Balance

In a relationship with a narcissist, it's easy to slip into a pattern in which you do more of the hard work than he does. Narcissists tend to be like Tom Sawyer—if you're not careful, you may find yourself painting a fence for him and then thanking him for the opportunity. I'm not suggesting that you keep a scorecard, tallying everything that he does and you do, such as chores or unpleasant things that must be tended to. However, it's wise to keep some perspective on just how much of the work of maintaining a relationship, a home, and perhaps a family each of you is doing. Be prepared to assert yourself in order to maintain some balance.

Assess Your Options

It may seem that being in a relationship with a narcissistic man is a lot of work. In truth, it can be, but only if your personality is the exact opposite of that of the narcissist. This does happen, since narcissists are often drawn to women who will meet their needs and support their inflated egos. In such a situation, a woman is apt to become the proverbial doormat and end up carrying around a lot of resentment.

However, if you are an unassertive, unassuming type, you do have other options. One is to stay away from narcissistic men (especially those whose narcissism is extreme) and seek out men who are more like you. An alternative, though, is to work on raising your expectations, asserting yourself to get what you want, and treating yourself (at least sometimes) like the special person you are.

Chapter Eighteen

Make Life with a Beach Boy a Two-Way Street

Millions of men and women love the singing group The Beach Boys, and I'm one of them. Their lighthearted, upbeat songs never fail to lift my mood whenever I hear one on the radio. But as much as people might enjoy and appreciate The Beach Boys for what they are, not many women would want to commit to a relationship with one.

The image of a beach boy is closely connected to the surfer culture that flourished in the 1960s and 1970s. It conjures up images of the carefree life, being close to nature, enjoying the rush that comes from riding a wave, and just plain having fun. It's a lifestyle that's nicely summed up in the phrase, "Surf's up!"

The beach boy is not without his virtues. He has a capacity for enjoying life, for silliness, and for lightheartedness. He doesn't take life too seriously. These are qualities that can bring joy and laughter into a relationship. If you see yourself as being an overly serious person whose life is dominated by responsibilities, then a beach boy could be very attractive to you.

Take That Nose off the Grindstone!

The beach boy personality may appeal to you if you're the kind of woman whose life could be summed up by the phrase "all work and no play." Many successful, hard-working women find themselves drawn into relationships with this type of man precisely because he has qualities they envy to some degree. Ironically, they usually end up working just as hard as (or harder than) they ever did, while the beach boy goes on enjoying life.

Jodi and CJ: Life with a Golfer

Jodi was one of those women you can't help but admire. Her father had worked two jobs, with never a word of complaint, in order to allow her mother to devote herself to raising four children, of whom Jodi was the oldest. Three of the four went on to college, and the fourth went to trade school. Jodi won an athletic scholarship that paid for all four years of her undergraduate education. She then went to graduate school to study social work, paying for it with work and student loans. After finishing graduate school, she got a job in a large state agency and, through a combination of diligence, hard work, and social skills, quickly moved up the chain of command. Now, at 36, she held a managerial position. She was making good money, and she liked her work.

Jodi met Charles—who went by his first and last initials, CJ—when she was in undergraduate school. CJ finished college as well, though just barely. He liked to joke that his major was "golf," which was actually more truth than joke. CJ liked golf like Casanova liked women—he couldn't get enough of it. In college, he wouldn't give a second thought to missing class on a good spring or fall day in order to hit the links. He was a decent, but not exceptional, golfer. He wasn't good enough to make the university's golf team, but he did know the game, and was good enough to be able to teach the basics to friends who expressed an interest.

CJ and Jodi dated through their senior year. After graduating, she enrolled in graduate school and lived with her parents to save money. CJ got a job with a large golf equipment company that had a number of stores and sold both wholesale and retail. Ostensibly interested in moving up to a managerial position, CJ started out as a salesman. Ten years later, he was still a salesman, albeit one of the company's most successful ones. During that time, he and Jodi got married and had a son.

For their first anniversary, Jodi surprised CJ with a set of beautiful clubs that cost her more than $2,000, even at the wholesale price she got them for. CJ was pleased, to say the least, and responded by playing golf more than ever. Because he worked on Saturdays, CJ had a day off during the week when Jodi was at work. With the exception of winter days when the course was closed, he would always play a full round of golf on his day off, after which he would hang out at the pro shop or the club house.

Through his job, CJ met many successful men who played golf, and he would regularly boast to Jodi and friends about all the people he knew in high places—lawyers, judges, surgeons, financial advisers, builders, and executives, to name a few. He counted them among his friends. Indeed, it did appear that CJ and his customers would often trade advice—what kind of putter to buy, for example, in exchange for advice about the best mutual funds to invest in.

Enough Is Enough

By the time their fifth anniversary rolled around, Jodi was beginning to chafe at the bit. Although she liked her work and did not resent it in the least, she was now making more than twice CJ's salary. Despite this disparity in wages, he enjoyed a full membership in a private golf club and owned his own golf cart. He played golf a minimum of twice a week, including virtually every Sunday, as well as his weekday off.

Jodi was especially bothered by the fact that between working every Saturday and golfing every Sunday for eight months of the year, CJ spent precious little time with his son outside of a few hours before bedtime. If she tried to raise the issue with CJ, however, he'd bristle. His pat reply was that when his son was old enough, he'd teach him to play golf.

Can you relate to Jodi's situation? Does it seem to you as though you are (or have been) in a relationship with a man who seems to have all the fun, while you do all the work? Were you ever attracted to a man precisely because he seemed to know how to enjoy life, while you regarded yourself as a bit of a drone?

Was CJ a "bad" man? Not really. He had never been deceitful about his love for golf. He golfed a lot, but he also held down a job. He hung out with friends at the clubhouse, but he never came home drunk. As far as Jodi knew, he'd never been unfaithful. Finally, though he earned a lot less than his wife did, insisted that his membership dues be paid from their joint account, and always had some "walking around money" in his pocket, CJ did have his paychecks deposited into their joint account. From his point of view, he was meeting his commitment to his marriage while still maintaining what he considered to be a healthy interest in golf.

Clearly, then, CJ was not a bad man—he was just a beach boy. The problem in the marriage was Jodi's, not CJ's. It would only become his problem if Jodi decided to divorce him. That, of course, was a possibility, though an unlikely one, given Jodi's deep sense of responsibility. But she began taking steps to build a life for herself and her son apart from CJ. She had, for example, joined a health club that had a daycare facility, so that she could exercise while her son played. She also decided to have an in-ground pool installed so that they could swim and entertain friends while

CJ golfed. This idea of building a life of her own, it turns out, is something a woman must seriously consider if she chooses to stay in a relationship like the one that Jodi found herself in.

Strategies for Living with a Beach Boy

Here are some specific dos and don'ts to consider if you decide that the man you are with has some of the beach boy personality in him. Of course, your chances of making such a relationship satisfying over the long run are better if he is not an extreme beach boy, but simply leans in that direction.

Don't Live Vicariously

Many women end up in a relationship with a man who has a beach boy personality simply because he is able to enjoy life and have fun, while she can't seem to give herself permission to do that. This is another example of how "opposites attract," and why it usually isn't a good idea to base a relationship on this notion. It's one thing for a couple to appreciate each other's strengths and what those strengths contribute to a relationship. It's another thing entirely to believe that you can fulfill yourself by living vicariously through someone else.

Look for a Man Who Shares your Work Ethic

Rather than trying to live vicariously and have fun through someone else, you are better off partnering with a man whose attitude toward work is similar to yours. Then, if you think that work is taking up too much of your life, you can work together toward the goal of a more balanced lifestyle.

Balance Fun with Serious Responsibilities

This is a corollary to previous advice. Instead of living vicariously, work toward the goal of creating some balance in your own lifestyle. If necessary, work with a counselor or a personal life coach to accomplish this.

Don't Encourage Irresponsibility

Encouraging a beach boy to be responsible is not the same as throwing a wet towel over his life. That is not likely to work anyway. However, don't repeat Jodi's mistake and get off on the wrong foot. When she bought CJ such an extravagant gift for their first anniversary, she was not only being generous but also was unwittingly giving him permission to play golf to his heart's content. Why would he think otherwise? If the man in your life has such an outside interest, you're better off from the beginning talking about how responsibilities would be divided between you, including how you will pay the bills, maintain a household, and so on, if you were to commit to each other. In doing so, you are not denying a man his fun; you are merely asserting the fact that a healthy lifestyle needs to balance fun and responsibility. A healthy adult—man or woman—can accept the fact that a person has to sometimes give up some personal fun for the sake of a relationship or a family; but that doesn't mean that he or she is being denied all fun.

Take a Class in Laughter

I'm not kidding. There are actually such classes, in which you can learn to tell a joke, act silly, or just plain laugh. If you're a person who can't seem to get a belly laugh going once in a while, look for such a class and sign yourself up. Believe it or not, being able to laugh will help you to loosen up in every way. It will also help you discover things to do that are fun. For some reason, I've found that people who say they don't know how to have fun also don't laugh a lot. The more you can do both of these things, the less you'll have to rely on someone else to do them for you.

Case Study

Sandy's Story: Making Her Own Fun

Here is how one woman broke through her barriers to having a balanced lifestyle. For 15 years, Sandy pretty much kept her nose to the grindstone. Since graduating from high school, education and work were the dominant themes in her life. She first put herself through nursing school and then earned a master's degree in nursing, all the while working full time. After that, she set a goal to become a licensed nurse practitioner, which took another two years of intensive study and preparation for a difficult test.

Finally, at age 34, Sandy found herself with some time on her hands, but she had no idea what she wanted to do with it. Her first thought was to set yet a further career goal, but another part of her resisted that strategy. That resistant part was actually her healthy self, struggling to get some air.

Sandy had a few relationships, virtually all of them with beach-boy types. Two of these men ended up living with her. They had a couple of things in common. All were good talkers, sociable and friendly men, who were comfortable in crowds. They also liked to have a good time, and made no secret of it. They all had jobs, but with the exception of one man who had a knack for selling expensive cars (and probably could have sold gas grills in hell), none of them made a lot of money. But they did know how to have fun, and they were able to persuade Sandy to spend some of her money doing things that they enjoyed. Typically, she enjoyed many of these activities as well, though she never actually chose them herself.

The thing that drew Sandy to these beach boys was the fact that she was, by nature, such a serious person. For example, though she had a good sense of humor, she rarely told a joke. She was frugal and had learned to plan far ahead when it came to finances. She spent little on herself, but had already amassed a sizable retirement account through the hospital where she worked. What the beach boys she got involved with brought to Sandy's life was a capacity to have fun that she just could not seem to find in herself.

When the third of these mismatches ended after two years, Sandy took a friend's advice and sought professional therapy. Her therapist sized her up after a single session. "You're an intelligent, hard-working, and successful woman," she told Sandy. "But somewhere along the way, you forgot to have a life. You have an opportunity to do that now, but I have to tell you that as easy as that may sound, it will not be easy for you to do. We will have to work together on that, and you will probably also need help from some women friends. And I *mean* women friends because the last thing you need to be doing at this point is looking to another irresponsible man to show you how to let your hair down and have a good time. I think you'll agree that you've been there, done that, more than once."

These brief comments succinctly captured Sandy's "treatment plan." Happily, over the next two years Sandy made significant headway in building the balanced life she had neglected for so long. She was fortunate to have several good women friends, who, like her, earned salaries that allowed them to indulge in some fun if they chose to do so. Sandy went on two great adventures with friends, a five-day rafting expedition down the Colorado River and a weeklong scuba-diving vacation. By the time the second adventure was over, Sandy had truly broken out of her old pattern of self-denial. She was now in a position to balance work with pleasure and, as a result, was less vulnerable to hooking up with a beach boy in order to achieve that end.

Assess Your Options

Following the guidelines presented in this chapter can help prevent a relationship with a man who has some of the beach boy in him from deteriorating over time into a one-way street. That's what happened to Jodi and could easily have happened to Sandy.

Remember that it's fine if you and the man in your life *both* have some of this in your personalities. They issue is not having fun; rather it is a matter of learning to live a balanced lifestyle.

If you are a workaholic, drawn to men who live their lives with a care-free spirit, you have options. One is to avoid beach boys (especially those whose attitude is all about fun) and seek out men who are more like you. An alternative, though, is to work on raising your expectations, clearly lay out how you will share the responsibilities of running a home and taking care of a family, and allow yourself (at least sometimes) to have fun times, too.

Chapter Nineteen

Avoiding the Web of Addiction

Al-Anon is a fellowship dedicated to providing support for those who find themselves in a relationship with an addict. One idea that a person often hears in Al-Anon goes something like this: "You didn't cause it, and you can't cure it." The "it," of course, refers to the addiction. Be it alcohol, drugs, gambling, work, or the Internet, addiction takes on a life of its own. Once it gets a foothold in a person's psyche, addiction progresses until it eventually takes control of that person's life.

Case Study

Cindy and Roberto: Facing Addiction Early

When Cindy's husband, Roberto, told her he decided to buy himself a high-end gaming computer so he could entertain himself with some of the games the fellows at work had told him about, she smiled and wrote it off to the boy in him. Like all men, Roberto liked his toys, and Cindy figured that this was just the latest one.

Roberto set up his computer and logged on to several simulated war games. Initially, he limited this activity to weekends, for just an hour or two at a time. Cindy had interests of her own—in particular, working out. They belonged to a health club and would go there together three times a week. In addition Cindy had a couple of hobbies of her own that she busied herself with while Roberto played on his computer.

After a couple of months, Cindy noticed that Roberto had all but stopped going to the health club. She mentioned it to Roberto, who just laughed and made a joke about becoming a "game addict." But he didn't leave his computer or resume going to the club more often. This bothered Cindy, but since she felt hard pressed to deny Roberto his obvious enjoyment and thought he would eventually lose interest in the war games, she opted to say nothing. That was her first mistake.

It wasn't long before Roberto couldn't wait to get home from work to pick up his battle plan where he'd last left it. Barely six months after he

Leave Your Guilt at the Door!

Guilt is the most common reason women get themselves into a position in which they actually promote a man's addiction, as opposed to helping stem it. This behavior, called *enabling,* is most often motivated by feelings of either guilt or fear. A woman may believe on some level that she is responsible for a man's addiction. Often, addicts promote this belief by telling their partners they are responsible. "If you were married to my wife you'd drink, too," goes the old joke. Only, it's all too often not a joke. A statement like that is intended to evoke guilt, which then causes the woman to do things that enable the addiction to continue.

The second reason women enable addiction has to do with fear. A woman who is married to an alcoholic may feel compelled to cover up for him out of fear of the financial or other practical consequences if she doesn't. This same kind of fear keeps many abused women from turning in their abusers. Keeping the idea, "You didn't cause it, and you can't cure it," in mind can be very helpful in getting past any guilt you may feel. You might even want to write it down and tape it in a place where you will see it every day.

bought his computer, he was playing his games late into the night, three or four times a week. Cindy, meanwhile, now found herself going to bed alone with a book to read. At that point, although Cindy didn't realize it, Roberto's relationship with his computer had progressed from that of a "friend" to that of a "relationship," though it had not yet become a "commitment." For example, if Cindy asked Roberto to come to bed for a "date"—their code word for sex—at that point he would still put his game on hold and come to bed, even though he might go back to it after they made love.

A year after getting his computer games, Roberto showed no signs of losing interest in them, as Cindy had hoped. On the contrary, she was feeling more lonely than ever and rather resentful of the computer, though she was still inclined to bite her tongue rather than create a scene. Another mistake. Roberto was now staying up until the wee hours of the morning on the computer. And if she brought up the idea of a "date" he was increasingly likely to put Cindy off, saying something like "I'll be there in a little while," and then would not show up.

The Commitment Stage

Roberto was addicted—he was *committed* to his computer. Meanwhile, like anyone who has been jilted, Cindy was getting weary and more resentful than ever. It was obvious to her, though Roberto denied it, that he had put his computer games ahead of their marriage—and almost everything else, other than his job.

Then came the final straw. One night when she was sleeping fitfully, Cindy heard Roberto go into the bathroom and close the door. It was a little after 3 am. Acting purely on instinct, she quietly slipped out of bed and padded into the spare room where Roberto had been playing on his computer. From across the room, she could see what looked like a picture of a woman. It was not pornography—the woman was dressed, and quite nicely at that. But she wasn't a real woman; rather, the image on the screen was a computerized image of a woman. Underneath this image was a message that began, "Rob, my love." As she looked closer, Cindy realized that these words were part of an ongoing dialogue between her husband and the fictional woman on the screen. Only the woman, despite the computerized image, seemed real, in that the dialogue appeared to be between two real people. Then Roberto came into the room.

Roberto moved from being addicted to computer war games to being addicted to Internet relationships. He never actually met any of the women he got to know this way. Rather, like him, the women (if they really were women!) he would meet on the Internet all had created personas that they used to act out their romantic and sexual fantasies. The supposed woman that Cindy saw on the screen that night was someone Roberto started "dating" only about a month earlier. They had not yet had cybersex but were in the process of getting to know one another and appeared to be falling in love.

Unfortunately, although Cindy and Roberto sought counseling and he vowed to give up his Internet addiction, he was not able to do so. A month after he said he was finished with it, Cindy discovered a laptop computer that Roberto had stashed away in the basement. On the pretext of doing some long-overdo household repairs, he would head down to his workbench after dinner each night, where he would hook up his computer and resume his Internet "dating."

Educate Yourself About Addiction

This book is a good introduction to understanding what addiction is and how it progressively overtakes an individual's life. Addiction does not emerge full-blown; rather, it begins as a small part of a person's life, and in that sense, is almost like a friend who brings pleasure or comfort. At that stage few people feel threatened by what could become an addiction. Over time, the *friend* progresses to a *relationship* and then to a *commitment*.

At the relationship stage, the emerging addiction begins to compete with the emerging addict's other priorities, including his relationship with you. You may begin to feel jealous, but you may also question whether you have a right to do so. This will most likely be the case if the addiction is a socially acceptable one, like Roberto's initial interest in online computer games, as opposed to an unacceptable one, such as drinking or gambling.

At the commitment stage, the activity not only competes with, but actually replaces, his commitment to you. At that point, jealousy usually gives way to outright resentment or alienation. If allowed to progress unchallenged, the one-time friend ultimately evolves into a master that controls the addict's life. Nothing else can compete with the demands of this master. At that point you have no relationship, and no choice but to draw a line in the sand, turn the tables, and give the addict a choice that you dictate: He needs to choose between the addiction and you. Even then, you should not get your hopes up unless you see more than words on his part.

Strategies for Coping with Addiction

Here are some guidelines to follow if you sense that the man in your life has addictive tendencies. As is true for all the chapters in this part of the book, these guidelines are offered on the assumption that this man did not score exceptionally high on the Addiction Index. It also assumes that he basically passes all four critical tests for relationships. In that case, the challenge you face is to not do things that will unwittingly promote (enable) his addiction. However, if he already appears to have slipped into addiction to the point where he is out of control (the commitment stage), you'd be wise to put away any rescue fantasies you may be indulging in and look elsewhere for a partner.

You Didn't Cause It, But You Can Make It Worse

This statement is not intended as a guilt trip, nor does it contradict the Al-Anon saying, "You didn't cause it, and you can't cure it." Rather, this statement reflects a simple realization of the fact that saying and doing nothing only allows addiction to progress from one stage to the next.

Of course, speaking up about what you see—an emerging addiction—is no guarantee that you will cure the addict. But that is better by far, for both of you, than keeping quiet.

Similarly, telling yourself that if you just love him enough you can free a man from an emerging addiction is not likely to work. Too many battered women have told themselves the same thing about loving an abusive man, in the hope that he would stop being abusive. Rather than telling yourself that you can cure a man of addiction, just tell yourself that you need to be honest and confront him every time you see evidence of it. Don't be quiet and tolerant, for example, if you notice that he is drinking more and more and falling asleep on the couch. Point it out, and let him know that you miss his company. By the same token, don't hesitate to say so if you think he is beginning to show more interest in the Internet, or the casino, than he shows in you.

Don't Become a Cushion!

"Raising the bottom" is an expression commonly used in Alcoholics Anonymous and Al-Anon. It refers to the things that people who are in relationships with addicts can do that will have the effect of forcing the addict to come to terms with the natural consequences of his addiction. Basically it means not allowing yourself to become someone who "cushions the blow," thereby allowing the addiction to continue or even get worse.

In the example, if Cindy had chosen to simply walk away from Roberto's computer when she discovered his online second life, that would have constituted being a cushion. By doing that she would have inadvertently allowed Roberto's addiction to continue, perhaps even to worsen. Instead, she confronted him and insisted that they seek help. That would be called "raising the bottom" because by doing so Cindy forced Roberto to face the consequences. Later on, when Roberto continued to choose his addiction over his marriage, Cindy chose to divorce him (another natural consequence of his addiction).

Another example would be a woman who discovers that her partner has a gambling problem and has just maxed-out his credit card at the casino—a natural consequence of his behavior. The best thing to do in that situation is to let him figure out how to get out of that jam. In contrast, fronting him the money or helping him figure out how to save his credit rating would be another example of cushioning the blow.

One woman made it clear that unless her fiancé was willing to place limits on the amount of time he devoted to research and shopping on the computer, she would seriously consider calling off their engagement. Another told her boyfriend, after he got drunk at a dinner party, that if he ever did that again she would simply disappear and drive home alone.

All of these actions are examples of allowing the addict to experience the natural consequences of his actions. In each example, it's easy to see how the women's actions are more likely to help arrest an addiction than promote it. Addicts typically are not motivated to give up their addiction until some serious consequences occur.

Cushioning an addictive man from the consequences of his addictive behavior is the most common mistake you can make in a relationship with an addict, but it is also the most difficult to resist. If your man's addiction is, in fact, pretty far along, you should seriously consider going to Al-Anon or a similar support group to help you build up your resistance to becoming a cushion, which typically has to do with fear of what will happen if you don't.

Assess Your Options

Living with a man who has some addictive tendencies requires a degree of vigilance, along with a willingness to do what needs to be done to avoid enabling addictive behavior. It is not, by any means, an impossible task, especially with a man who has not yet shown any signs of loss of control. Perhaps he just seems to have an excessive interest in something. If they take some time to think about it, most women can identify what stage a man is in, from friendship to relationship to commitment.

The times we live in are definitely conducive to men and women alike overdoing just about anything you can think of, and therefore, of slipping into a lifestyle that is out of balance. It is quite possible to avoid this if you can find it in yourself to face up to it, rather than avoiding early signs that trouble you on a gut level. Paying attention to what your gut is telling you can be vital to a relationship.

Chapter Twenty

How to Live with a Control Freak

Here, again, is an example of a "problem man" whom many women, once they identify him, may want to avoid altogether. But there are degrees of control, just as there are degrees of insecurity and narcissism, and just as there are stages of addiction. One of the keys to maintaining a relationship with a man who may not yet be a true control freak but has the potential to become one is to "speak truth to power," meaning to summon up the courage to speak up for yourself even to someone who can be intimidating.

The biggest mistake in a relationship is to make a habit of allowing issues of control to pass—in other words, to give in rather than risk a conflict. Especially early on, the woman who is too eager to have a relationship may decide to yield. She may tell herself something like, "It's no big deal. Let him have it his way." She may even believe that she is helping to make the relationship work by minimizing conflict—in other words, by "not being a bitch." She may have read something that advised her that the key to happiness is to let a man be in control all the time.

Don't Fear the "B" Word

The most common reason women back off from confronting a man who is too preoccupied with control goes back to ancient stereotypes about women and how a proper woman should behave. For too long some men have tried to shame women or get them to back down in a confrontation by calling them a "bitch." It's really surprising that so many women are willing to tolerate this. If you have done this, do yourself a favor and think long and hard about the implications of putting up with this behavior. Are you willing to be called a bitch? Are you really someone who lives to make a man miserable, or are you only a bitch when he doesn't like what you're saying to him, or when you won't simply back down and give him his way?

Strategies For Managing the Need to Control

If the man in your life has some tendencies to be controlling, but is not (at least not yet) a true control freak, there are things you can do to help prevent that from happening.

Understand What It's About

Generally speaking, the need to control is driven by anxiety. Some people try to control anxiety by compulsively cleaning, while others do it by attempting to control things. That's why most control freaks get upset if they have to change their plans or if their routine gets thrown off.

Chances are that you've known women who have had an eating disorder like anorexia. Such a disorder is also driven by anxiety. The anorexic woman is frustrated by all the things she can't control in her life, so she settles on something she can control—her weight. But her desire to control her weight goes way beyond normal dieting. The anorexic actually feels anxious and guilty if she eats. She controls her anxiety by not eating. Of course there are severe negative consequences associated with this way of controlling anxiety.

When you look at a man who has a tendency to be controlling, keep in mind that underneath his need to control things is probably some significant anxiety. You may have no idea where the anxiety originally came from, but it will be much better in the long run for both of you if you don't give in to it. Instead, let him deal with it.

Case Study

Lisa and David: An Escape Story

David's obsession with control began in late childhood and has been a powerful force in his life ever since. He was the oldest of three children and, like many in his position, he grew up trying to be good. He described his father as a basically happy, optimistic man. But he also worked the second shift for most of David's life, and consequently, David and he had relatively little contact. David's mother, meanwhile, seemed to come from a family whose general attitude toward life was fearful and pessimistic. David recalled how she often expressed concern that something bad might befall the family. "Especially when something good would happen," David told me. "Then she'd be even more likely to express a fear that disaster could be just around the bend!"

Between his own desire to be good and his mother's fear of calamity, David was an anxious child who controlled his anxiety through rituals and compulsive behaviors. He described himself as a "neat freak" whose room was always in order. Before going to sleep at night, he would have to recite a series of prayers in a precise order. At school, he was fearful of getting a wrong answer or doing anything that might possibly get him into trouble. Fortunately, he was a bright child and earned good grades. But David described himself on the inside as "a bundle of nerves."

David met Lisa when they were in their early 30s. He previously had a few, fairly brief relationships; she had several long-term ones, including one engagement that ended when she realized her fiancé was an incurable ladies' man. At the time they met, David's anxieties happened to be at an all-time low. A teacher, he liked his work and was good at it. He was also experienced, having taught the same grade for several years, and so he had his curriculum pretty much down pat.

Although he was by no means debilitated by anxiety, David nonetheless still maintained a number of rituals, led a very routine life, and kept his life in order. Under such circumstances, life was actually quite manageable, even enjoyable for him. However, beneath the relatively calm exterior that Lisa first got to know and found attractive was the same old anxiety that plagued David as a youth.

The Tale of the Potted Plant

When she first bumped up against David's need to be in control, Lisa didn't know quite what to make of it. They'd been dating steadily for about ten months and had come to spend more and more time visiting each other in their condos. The first sign of control that caught Lisa's attention was actually minor: She moved a potted plant in David's living room from the spot in a shaded area where David had set it to the center of a table where bright light streamed in through a bay window. When she visited again two days later, she noticed that the plant was back in its shaded spot. She casually pointed out to David that the plant would do better in the sunnier spot, but he shrugged and said, "That's okay, I like keeping it there." He didn't seem concerned about the plant or its need for sun—the issue for him was where it belonged.

After the potted plant incident, Lisa started noticing how everything in David's house indeed appeared to have its place. Initially, she just thought he was a neat person, which she appreciated. Then she realized that it went beyond neat. If she inadvertently put something in a different spot, it would quickly reappear where it had originally been. Not wanting to make a fuss for no good reason, she opted to put this observation on hold. In the back of her mind, though, she did wonder what might happen if she and David were to live together. She felt that she could tolerate David's need to have everything in its place, when it was *his* place. But living together would be a different matter entirely: If it were *their* place, she told herself, a potted plant would definitely be in the sun.

As you might have guessed, Lisa would have been better off confronting David's need to control early on, even over the seemingly innocuous plant incident. That might have been an easy battle for her to win, as well as establishing a pattern in her relationship with David. It would have told him that he would need to take Lisa's ideas and desires into account, and not just give in to his obsession with control. Instead, Lisa avoided bringing up the issue until after she moved in with David.

Sadly for David, his relationship with Lisa lasted barely six months after she moved in. Fortunately for her, she decided not to put her own condo up for sale. Instead, she sublet it for six months to give her some time to see how things would go between them. Maybe on some gut level she had her reservations. It was a good thing she decided to trust them when David initially suggested that she sell her condo and bank the profit.

It was not until after she moved in, when she saw him on a daily basis, that it became painfully clear to Lisa that the least little disruption in David's hyper-organized and hyper-routine world could send him into a tailspin. He would instantly become moody or irritable if she attempted to do just about anything *her* way.

David's obsession with control infected virtually every aspect of his life. He appeared relaxed and happy only when (and because) he had everything under control. There was no room, however, for someone else's personality to coexist in David's life. As Lisa discovered to her dismay, David was a very anxious person at heart. He worried excessively about almost anything. Like his mother, he had an irrational and vague fear of impending doom. His main means of relieving his anxiety was to obsessively control just about everything in his life. Lisa knew that, sooner or later, she would feel smothered in such a relationship, so she bit the bullet, ended it, and escaped before she got in too deep.

Have Some Things Your Way

From the very outset of any relationship you choose to pursue, make a point of asking to have some things your way. Not everything, mind you, but some things. This is a simple but effective way to test for the possibility that a man may be too much into control. It's also a good precedent to establish from the start. Here are a few concrete suggestions:

- As Lisa did in the example, try moving something minor from one spot to another, simply saying that you like that object and want to see how it might look in a different spot. If he shrugs it off and seems okay with the move, take that as a positive sign.
- Suggest going to a new place to eat at the last minute. See if he can tolerate at least that amount of spontaneity.
- Cook a meal for him at his place and see if he can keep himself from trying to manage everything or offer unsolicited advice while you're cooking.
- If you are getting serious about the relationship, mention one thing to him that you would change if you lived together. For example, if you would like to change the color of the bathroom, say so, and see how he responds.
- Tell him that you're going to make plans for what you will do together one weekend afternoon and see if he is comfortable with you being in control on that occasion.
- Insist on being the one who drives sometimes when you're going out together and then take a route you choose. Does this bug him, or is he able to sit back and enjoy the ride?

Express Your Opinions—See if He Can Agree to Disagree

At times, make a point of calmly but clearly letting him know about it when you disagree with him or have a different opinion about something. This almost qualifies as another critical test for a good relationship. The chances of having a good relationship over the long run are virtually nil unless two people are able to acknowledge their occasionally divergent tastes or opinions—in other words, to agree to disagree.

It goes without saying that a good relationship is built on a lot of common ground, but there needs to be some room for diversity as well. On the one hand, if you find yourself frequently biting your tongue and not expressing your opinion, take that as a bad omen. On the other hand, if you discover that you can enjoy a lively, respectful airing of differences and come to understand your respective opinions with no hard feelings, you may very well have a keeper.

Assess Your Options

All of these "tests" for checking out a man are also good rules for building a good relationship. It can be tempting for some women to let a man take charge, especially women who feel that they are burdened with too many responsibilities and have to make too many decisions—for instance, single mothers. Part of them may yearn for that old-fashioned kind of "take charge" man. The award-winning western *Shane* is about a man like that. It's an old film, but it's worth seeing if you're a single mother.

A good relationship is based on sharing the load, not putting it on one person's shoulders. That also means sharing in the decision-making process. Some couples still seem to prefer a more traditional splitting of responsibilities—for example, with one person being the primary bread-winner and the other having primary responsibility for housekeeping and childrearing.

Some men have moved into the latter role, becoming stay-at-home dads, while the wife brings home the bacon. This arrangement is still somewhat unusual, though. More commonly, women who are mothers have to both work outside the home and do the lion's share of the household tasks and childrearing. It is the rare father who knows who his child's pediatrician is or has taken the child to see that doctor. Fathers also remain relatively uninvolved in decisions surrounding their children's education. If you are seeking a truly balanced relationship, initiate an ongoing dialogue about these nuts-and-bolts aspects of parenting and how you will make decisions in these areas together.

To moderate a man's tendencies to control everything in his life, you must be prepared to persevere in doing all of the little things described above. Though moving a vase, or even buying a new one and placing it where you like it, may seem like a small thing. In fact, it is these little things that can make a big difference in the long run. The more successful you are at making these little cracks in a man's rigid lifestyle, the more likely it is that the relationship could work for you in the long run.

Chapter Twenty-One

Coping with a Predatory Man

The title of this chapter might strike you as ominous. Does it really make any sense to talk about coping with a predatory man? Wouldn't it be better to just turn and run the other way as fast as you can?

My response is that for some women, it actually can make sense to be in such a relationship, depending on two things: just how predatory the man is, and just how assertive, self-assured, and outspoken you are.

Many of the traits described in Chapter Eleven on predatory men are actually qualities that can make for success in today's competitive world. Most successful CEOs and entrepreneurs, for instance, have at least a little of the predator in them (and the unscrupulous ones have a lot). However, in the most successful businessmen these traits are balanced by good communication skills and the ability to inspire teamwork.

If, in your honest opinion, you are a particularly unassertive or a fairly insecure woman, then a relationship with a man with even a moderate predatory streak is definitely not right for you. You're better off sticking with that honest assessment of yourself (instead of trying to be the woman you wish you could be) and avoiding such men. For you, this kind of relationship is very likely to turn into a one-way street in the man's favor. He will end up getting as much as he wants, and you will get very little, unless what you want just happens to coincide with what he wants as well.

However, a man who has a touch of the predator may in fact be a keeper for you if you see yourself with the following traits:

- You know what you want and are willing and able to assert yourself to get it.
- You can set goals and pursue them aggressively.
- You do not hesitate to speak your mind.

In fact, you may have found over time that less aggressive men tend to bore you, or you may have had the experience of eventually walking all over them. Some women may choose to be with a predatory man precisely because he is aggressive in getting what he wants, and this aggressiveness matches their own personality and offers the promise of a desirable lifestyle. Some might argue that this is playing with fire, but if you go into such a relationship with your eyes open, you will be less likely to get burned.

Case Study

Paloma and Cory: A Good Match

Paloma admitted that not everyone could take her personality. Even her best friends at times would joke about how she could put people off. From her point of view, though, she was simply a frank person who spoke her mind. She would "tell it like it is," to use her words. Indeed, when she would describe someone she disliked or a situation she found unacceptable, in no way could Paloma ever be accused of "sugar-coating" anything.

In the world of work, Paloma's personality had been a mixed blessing. She had an unusual job for a woman: Having earned a degree in engineering, she was a project supervisor on large construction projects. Along with two or three other on-site supervisors, Paloma's job was to see that buildings were built to specification, within budget, and on time. In that role, it paid to be forceful and direct, if not downright blunt about what had to be done, how it had to be done, and when it had to be done. Over the years, Paloma earned a reputation for being able to dish it out as well as anyone. Moreover, the projects she was assigned to were usually completed on time, according to specifications, and on budget. A few times, though, Paloma had been called on the carpet for being too gruff with the company's customers or subcontractors.

As functional as it was on the work site, Paloma's personality had never been an asset in her intimate life. It seemed that the men she met just didn't appreciate her style of relating. More than once, she was told that she was pushy, a know-it-all, or too headstrong for her own good. Depending on who was doing the talking and how she felt about him, such remarks either rolled off Paloma's back or hurt her deeply. She considered herself to be a caring, loving person, but also someone who didn't suffer fools lightly. As she put it, "I have a good bullshit detector, and I can't just turn it on when I leave for work in the morning, then turn it off when I'm on my way home."

Paloma was an aggressive, outspoken person, but in no way was she a predatory woman, and she was right to say that she was a caring person. She was loved by her family, who accepted both sides of her personality. Sure, she could be gruff and outspoken, but she was also thoughtful, loving, and generous. She never forgot a friend's or relative's birthday, and though she was not extravagant, her gifts never failed to please. These qualities notwithstanding, Paloma was obviously not the kind of person who would be the right partner for just any man.

Paloma's *Mr. Right* turned out to be a man whose personality over-lapped hers in many ways. He owned his own business. It was a smaller construction company than the one that Paloma worked for, and it regu-larly did work as a subcontractor for hers. His business was by no means small, however, and it had a reputation for doing things right and, like Paloma, was known for finishing its projects on time and within budget. His name was Cory.

A Question of Degree

Paloma had known Cory for several years on a professional level. Understandably, they got along well. Cory would laugh when Paloma cut loose with a diatribe about another subcontractor and his substandard work ethic, wastefulness, or inability to get things done on time.

Cory had some predatory qualities. Not that he was a stalker or some-one who preyed on vulnerable people for his own advantage. However, he was unapologetically a fierce competitor when it came to his business. He would keep his ears to the rails, as the expression goes, to try to antic-ipate what his competitors might be up to. He would then try to beat them to the punch whenever possible with a faster, less costly proposal for a project. Similarly he would not hesitate to lure a key employee away from a competitor in order to get an advantage in a competitive bidding process. And he never felt sorry for a competitor who lost out to him or for an employee he had to let go, either for lack of work or poor work habits. "I'm not a social service agency," he explained. "I'm a businessman."

Paloma and Cory started dating when she accepted his invitation to have lunch to celebrate the completion of a project. Paloma learned then that that Cory had been divorced for several years and was not dating.

Cory discovered, to his pleasant surprise, that outside of the context of her work, Paloma was someone who loved to have fun, could be silly, and was well read and broad-minded. For her part, Paloma discovered that as aggressive as Cory could be when it came to running his busi-ness, that was not all there was to him. Though he had no children of his own, Cory clearly had a lot of affection for several teenage nieces and nephews; he was generous with them and he looked out for them. He would help them, for example, find summer jobs, and had offered to match two-for-one any money they saved toward acquiring things they wanted—a car, an iPod, even a college education.

Paloma and Cory clearly appreciated each other's directness, and each respected the way the other handled themselves professionally. At the same time, they learned that outside of work they were both capable of letting their hair down. When she accepted an invitation to accompany Cory on a holiday visit to his family, Paloma saw a man who was totally relaxed and happy, and who was also obviously loved and respected.

It was the things they shared—their sense of humor, their openness to differences, their mutual respect, and their capacity for being caring and kind as well as aggressive and cut-and-dried—that eventually led to this being a good match. Cory turned out to be a keeper for Paloma, and vice versa.

Strategies for Living With a Predatory Man

Here are some things to contemplate if you think the man you are interested in has some predatory characteristics, and if you are trying to decide whether this relationship is worth investing in.

Learn to Identify the Predators to Avoid

This first guideline is far and away the most important one. All of the ones that follow are offered with this proviso—namely, that the man is not a severe predator. This means learning to take stock of a man who may have some of the predator in him. He should have a score of no more than 50 on the Predator Inventory in Chapter 11. He should also (at least minimally) pass all four critical tests for relationships. Men who are more predatory than that are best avoided—no matter how seductive they may be. In a word, don't let yourself become bait. In particular, avoid any man who expresses the belief that common-sense rules of conduct don't apply to him, or that it is okay to break a law as long as you don't get caught.

Know What Your Negatives Are and Accept Them

Some women argue that they should not have to build a thicker skin in order to have a relationship. They believe that in a good relationship, each partner is sensitive to the other's vulnerabilities and does not exploit them. If this is your belief, then you should avoid even moderately predatory men. However, some women are not opposed to the idea of learning to be less vulnerable. To survive in a relationship with a man like Cory, you would be smart to know not only what your personal strengths and assets are, but also to be aware of what your "negatives" are and to come to terms with them.

By *negatives,* I mean qualities in you that others may sometimes dislike. Paloma knew, for example, that others sometimes thought of her as prickly and brash. On the job, she'd been accused more than once of being difficult to get along with and too pushy. If she felt that these were bad traits, then she would have felt wounded when people said such things about her. She would have been motivated to suppress this part of her personality so that people would like her. In a relationship, this could lead to Paloma being on the defensive.

But Paloma came to accept that she could be a demanding perfectionist and at times more blunt than people cared for. She decided that she preferred that reputation to being liked but doing a poor job or to inhibiting her tendency to be outspoken in order to avoid ruffling others' feathers. She was who she was—if a man didn't like those qualities in her, as far as she was concerned, that was his problem.

What are your negatives in terms of how others see you? Think about each of the following areas of your life and rate each one from –10 (most negative) to +10 (most positive). For example, if you believe that others see you as easy to get along with, score yourself between +1 and +10. If you think people see you as someone who is difficult to get along with, score yourself between –1 and –10, depending on how difficult you've been told you are to get along with.

_____	Intelligent	_____	Trustworthy
_____	Attractive	_____	Relaxed
_____	Easy to get along with	_____	Friendly
_____	Likable	_____	Open-minded
_____	Good sense of humor	_____	Fun-loving
_____	Successful	_____	Flexible
_____	Physically fit	_____	Tolerant

Now look over your ratings. Breaking down your personality into individual characteristics and rating them objectively will help you understand yourself and how others see you.

The purpose of this exercise is not to drag you down or to suggest that only a woman with no negatives can have a successful relationship. Far from it. The point is that we all have our negatives. No one is a +10 in every way, at least not if they are being honest with themselves.

We can think of our negatives as potential vulnerabilities, and we can do one of two things about them:

1. Expect the people in our lives to avoid ever doing or saying anything that might bring up one of our negatives and make us feel bad. That's a variation on the line from the film *Love Story*—"Love means never having

to say you're sorry." To most people, that's a completely unrealistic idea. To live that way would require two perfect people.

2. Accept the idea that we have positives and negatives—that we are who we are—and not be ashamed of it. We can then try to correct our faults. At the same time, accepting who you are can help make you less vulnerable to manipulation. If someone tells you that you are a critical person, you can simply reply, "Yes, I am."

Be Pushy!

How would you react if someone said you were a "pushy" woman? Would that make you cringe? Or would your response be that you can indeed be pushy at times, and that's okay with you? In order to have a fulfilling relationship with an aggressive man—one in which you each get some of what you want—you also need to be able to be pushy at times. If you aren't, you will most likely end up holding the short end of the stick. Again, some women may feel that they either shouldn't have to be so assertive or that they just don't want to be. That's fine. In that case, avoid aggressive men. But if you want to pursue such a relationship, then you'll be better off if you are either naturally like Paloma or if you decide to make a concerted effort to be more comfortable being assertive.

Assess Your Options

Men like Cory are not the easiest men to have a mutually satisfying relationship with. Most such men end up either in relationships with meek women for whom they eventually lose respect or, like him, divorced. Cory was lucky that he found a good match in Paloma.

The choice is yours. Factors to consider include just how predatory a man is—is he predatory with you, or just in some situations, like work?— and whether he can pass the four critical tests for relationships. Don't choose such a man just because you wish you could be more like him. And be prepared to be pushy and outspoken at times in order to get your share of the pie. If you can do that, an aggressive man might just be a keeper.

Having read and taken time to digest the information in this book, you still may wonder whether you are being too picky if you follow the approach advocated here. Or you may wonder if it takes too dim a view of men. The answer to both questions is a resounding No! And my advice remains: Stop marketing yourself and start being selective!

That doesn't mean you should not make an effort to stay fit or make yourself attractive. On the contrary, I tell my male clients the same thing that I tell my female clients: Complacency is the enemy of a good relationship. Taking care of your health and your appearance is not only one way to attract others, but is also vital to keeping the spark alive in a relationship once you find it. However, that's not the same thing as treating yourself as if you were a commodity that you are trying to sell.

Keep in mind that the way you have learned to take stock of a man here recognizes that relatively few men meet the criteria for being a "problem man" in the extreme. Like yourself, the men you meet will not be perfect. On the other hand, the greater risk is to view all potential relationships through rose-colored glasses—to try to put a positive spin on a man's qualities or behavior that, in truth, make you feel at least a bit uneasy. Too many women waste entirely too much of their valuable time taking this Pollyannaish approach.

Knowing which one (or two) of the personality types discussed in Part Two best describes a man you are interested in places you in a position to avoid making a potentially small issue into a major one. It will give you a heads-up about what issues you can reasonably expect to crop up should you decide to pursue this relationship. Similarly, knowing which critical tests a man passes with flying colors, versus which ones he tends to stumble on, puts you in a position to ask for what you want. If he's stingy, for example, you can work on asking him for things you'd like. One woman did just that. She told her very frugal but also responsible and empathic boyfriend early on that she really liked him, but one thing that had always been very important to her was that any man in her life be sure to remember her birthday, and buy her flowers and a nice gift. The point got across, with the result that a potential problem was neatly circumvented, and the relationship moved on.

Many women have told me that they believe they can size up a man and spot potential keepers based on a single date. If that is true, great. But my advice to single women looking for a relationship has been the same advice that I give to single men: Unless something seems way off right from the start, don't rush to judgment. Whereas simple sexual attraction can be a spark that is present (or not) in a relationship right away, it may take some time for you to determine just how many critical tests for relationships a given man passes. It will also probably take more than a single date to get a full, three-dimensional view of a man's personality.

Rather than making you too picky or giving you a pessimistic view of men, think of the material in this book as a guide for what to look for in a man. It can save you time and heartache by helping you to see a man as he really is—to make an honest assessment of a man's personal assets as well as his liabilities. We all have our flaws, but what we seek in a partner is someone who possesses the character traits that are most important to us, and whose personality is basically compatible with our own. Taking the time to apply the knowledge you have acquired here will help you do just that. And you may find your keeper!

Index